My Sheep
Hear my Voice

My Sheep
Hear my Voice

A MEMOIR WITH AN AWESOME GOD

by Consuella Canada

TATE PUBLISHING *& Enterprises*

Published by Tate Publishing & Enterprises, LLC
127 E. Trade Center Terrace | Mustang, Oklahoma 73064 USA
1.888.361.9473 | www.tatepublishing.com

Tate Publishing is committed to excellence in the publishing industry. The company reflects the philosophy established by the founders, based on Psalms 68:11,
"The Lord gave the word and great was the company of those who published it."

Book design copyright © 2007 by Tate Publishing, LLC. All rights reserved.
Cover design by Jennifer L. Fisher
Interior design by Lynly D. Taylor

Published in the United States of America

ISBN: 978-1-60247-569-4
1. Christian Living   2. Recovery: Women
3. Spiritual Growth: Prayer

07.10.10

I dedicate this memoir to my Lord and Savior Christ Jesus.
For Your total faithfulness which allowed me to stand on
Your promises of faith, comfort, healing, strength and love.
Thank You for living Your life inside of me.
Your Friend, Your Sister and Co-heir to the throne, Consuella

To my Grandparents
Your prayers have shaped my life, and
without your faith, guidance, and love
there would be no me.

Rosa Lucinda Brown

Lawson L. Williams

Bessie Beatrice Brown Williams

Martha Nelson Dupree

Matthew Nelson

Martha Nelson

ACKNOWLEDGEMENTS

My God daddy, James Denlock Smith, Jr.

To my Husband, Claude W. Canada, Sr., thanks for all you have done to help maintain my health and strength. God saw you even as I didn't and what He saw proves that He is an all knowing God. Thank you for seeking God and for taking your rightful place in our family. I love you.

To my mother and stepfather, Fredrick and Edmonia Crowder, There are no words to express the love and care that you have given not only to me but my family. I thank you both for taking care of me when I couldn't do it for myself, I love you.

To my father and stepmother, Jeff and Lois Nelson, thank you for your prayers and support I love you.

To my children, Claude, Jr., Phileta, Kim, Marnia, Stevon, Tarrell, Alex, Marcellus, Jordan and my son-in-law, Reggie, you have been witnesses to God's power first hand never ever forget His faithfulness to answer prayers. Continue to seek the Lord and He will show you the way, I love you all very much.

To my grandchildren, Jasmine, Taylor and Mikai, you have opened a place in my heart that I didn't know existed until the day you were born. You have prepared my heart with prayer for my future grandchildren and the generations to come. Ganny loves you and remember prayer changes things.

To my sister and brother-in-law, Florence and Chris, I thank God for our relationships you are the epitome of what God says we should be for one another in more ways than one; I love you.

To my brother and sister-in-law, Reggie and Clara, as you grow together seek the Lord often, He will faithfully bring you through. I love you.

To my aunt Monzella Dorsey, I love you very much. Thank you for your prayers and support.

To my Uncle Horatio and Sister Jackie, thank you both for all of your support and love.

To my aunts and uncles, Martha, Leitha, Mary, Rotha Jr. Bill, Goldie, Rita, Richard and Great Aunt Rosalee, thank you all for welcoming me with opened arms, love you all!

To my nieces and nephews, Ramon, Jr., Lenea, Leonda, Reggie, Corey and Marcus, Aunt Connie loves you all very much.

To my cousins and their children, hold on to God. I thank Him for our relationships, I love each and every one of you.

To my godmother, June Brown, I love you and I thank you for all that you've done for me. God bless you!

To my god-daughter, Brittany, I love you and I still pray for you every day.

To Mr. and Mrs. Edwin Haynes, thank you so very much for accepting me into your family, May God bless you always.

To all of my family near and far, thank you for your prayers over my life, I love you all.

To my mother-in-law, Marie, brothers-in-law, Leslie and Larry, and sister-in-law, Lola, I thank God for placing us on the same path together. I love you.

To my second grade teacher, Mrs. Mandy Bynum, thank you and I will love you forever.

To Greg, thank you for everything.

To my pastor and first lady at St. Stephens, Rev. William A. Gray III and Rev. Candace Gray, may God continue to bless you; I thank you for your prayers!

To the ministers at St. Stephens, I pray that God may continue to use you for the management of His Kingdom. Thank you for your prayers and love.

To my church family, we must hold tight to the word of God,

I thank Him for allowing me to share the last seven years of my life with you, I thank God often for His radiating love that is here, in His people.

To St. Stephens Bible study class 2–7 and 8–12 years, for all of your prayers for me to walk, God has answered your prayers. Never forget that, I know I won't. I love you all!

To the kingdom of God, we must truly get to work that we may be ready when Christ returns!

To all nurses, nurse techs, my family and I celebrate you; we thank God for your commitment and love for people. You have comforted us, given us hope and were very patient even when we may have been angry and bitter with grief. You are the guiding lights, the shining stars for which we depend when we're not well. Thank you all!

To doctors, I thank you, remember to keep us (your patients) first, we depend on you for our healthy lives. God uses you to perform some of His greatest work.

To therapists: PT, OT, Respiratory, thank you for choosing your profession in service to teach us those valuable skills that trials and tribulations strip from us. You are all amazing.

To the staff of Sandalwood Elementary School, thank you for your continued support of my family, especially my young children. I don't have the words to express the gratitude for the love that flowed from within the hearts of the staff. Thank you, you will never be forgotten.

The Maryland General Home Health: Thank you all for your love and care both in my hospitalizations and at home, I will never forget any of you…ever.

The Brywn Mahr Rehabilitation Center, I thank each of you for your love and care and for assisting me at one of the weakest points of my life and I will pray for you always.

Mother Hattie Bright, God sent you to me after Ma-Ma died. You have encouraged me and often with the same words that my grandmother used. You began where she left off in my life and God allowed you to see me through His eyes. For all the prayers we've prayed, the words of assurance and all that you bring to my life, I thank God for you.

To my Evangelism Explosion instructor and his wife, Bro. Jeff and Sis. Lisa Stone, thank you for assisting me in recognizing my true calling.

To Mr. Joe and Mrs. Donna Walters, Mr. Brent Miller and Miss. Amber Yates, thank you for your love and support.

To all who have prayed and stood with me until the completion of this project: Thank you and continue to pray for me and with me.

Special Thanks to my Reviewers:
Rev. William A. Gray III
Mother Hattie Bright
Sister Florence Vaughan
Sister Maryann Flowers
Rev. William James
Sister Joanne Stone
Sister Lucille Jennings

TABLE OF CONTENTS

FROM THE DESK OF
MRS. MANDY BYNUM

As a retired elementary school teacher, I've long believed that love, patience, and a genuine caring are very important while shaping young minds.

In my second grade class my students were my children. Things were quite different then, a hug was just a hug, and a pat on the back was just a pat on the back. These went a long way to encourage children.

Though Consuella had limitations, my personal goal was to include her in all activities. I did not want her to feel any differently than any of my other children. Consuella displayed great interests in writing and art even then. Today I doubt that I would have been allowed to carry a child up and down the stairs, but if that act has left a positive and lasting impression I am thankful.

Teachers, we must be positive role models for our young people, whose lives have been entrusted to us for much of their day. Children will remember your love, patience and genuine caring, and that should be our goal.

Mrs. Mandy Bynum
Consuella's second grade teacher

INTRODUCTION

My Sheep Hear My Voice: A memoir with an Awesome God, is a very real and accurate account of my personal life experiences. It is a testimony of seeking God and finding Him within my personal relationship with Jesus. It is a testimony of a faithful God who never breaks a promise.

My testimony is very graphic at times, this is to bring clarity to the depth of my illnesses, that you may understand where God came to reach me. Prayerfully this will also encourage you in knowing and believing where He will come to reach you. I believe that in order for you to completely understand my story, you must go where I have been. You must feel some of what I have felt, the good and the bad. In today's world we need hard hitting evidence of God's presence. Just as some may hit hard as to discredit our God, we too must hit hard to prove His existence and His loyalty. Please know that for you it will be over at the end of the first chapter. For me it has been a lifetime, but I thank God, that He was there. My story features our awesome God at work with clear and convincing evidence.

My prayer is that though this is my personal story, you take time to look at the defining moments in struggles, hurt and pain to recognize our Creator's hand in your own lives. In my memoir, I chose to use life changing experiences as individual testimonies. I make comparisons to Jesus' life, in no way to imply that we are equal with Him; because of course we are not. Jesus was God. However I do make them according to the scriptures call for our lives. We must take responsibility for our own personal relationships with Christ. Our life's goal should be to strive to become more like Him.

As I grow in Christ-like character, and in God's love, I have become a witness to His Awesomeness. I will not only lift praises from my mouth, but also from my life. I want to reflect Him in my actions. God has done great things for each of us, and we must use our testimonies to encourage others, that they may also have hope and trust in Him.

This is my testimony; it is what I was allowed to experience in my life. These things would help me as I began to be transformed into His likeness. This is my quest to become who God had created me to be.

MY TESTIMONY/THE PROCESS

On May 16, 1956, I was born at the University of Maryland hospital. There the pediatricians discovered a VSD (Ventricle Septal Defect) a hole in my heart. Surgery was postponed until I was older. My mother was told that without surgery I would not survive past the age of sixteen.

I was not allowed to have a childhood of running, jumping rope or any other strenuous activity. Under the careful and watchful eyes of my Father God and the pediatricians, the surgery was scheduled when I was seven years old. It was announced on radio, TV and even a call to military bases for donations of blood for my surgery.

I was admitted to the hospital on the day after Thanksgiving, and was being prepared for surgery with many tests and procedures. "Do you know what we are going to do today Consuella?" Dr. Davis asked.

"I have a hole in my heart and you, and the other doctors are going to fix it," I answered. On the morning of the surgery I heard my mom crying, I wanted to hug her as I was being rolled away from my room to the elevator. I knew that she would sleep in my room with me she did that a lot. I was given medication before I left my room that made me feel drowsy.

I remember a dream where I looked down on the doctors and nurses working on my heart. Then a dream that I played with angels I could feel that they loved me, we were rolling and tumbling in the clouds, and they made me laugh. Then in another dream I was told that Santa was coming to see me. I was kept under sedation with the aid of medication for two weeks. I remember opening my eyes and a nurse rushed over.

"My goodness I'm glad to see those eyes opened, your mother just left. I'm going right to that phone, and let her know that you're awake," she said as she took my vital signs.

There was tubing down my throat and I couldn't talk. Then I looked around and there were so many machines surrounding me. When my mom came in she had lots of hugs and kisses from everyone. After a few days I was moved to a room, and my mom brought cards from my sister Shelly and my brother Jerry. My best friends Karen and Charles; and my second grade teacher and classmates sent letters and cards.

Santa came to the hospital and brought so many toys for my new friends and me. I went home the same day which was the day before Christmas Eve and I shared my toys with Shelly, Jerry and my cousins.

I had a tutor until I was able to go back to school in March 1964, but I could not walk the stairs or participate in physical education. It was suggested that I be sent to another classroom during recess, but Mrs. Taylor wouldn't hear of it. I was a part of her class even when in recess and she carried me up and down two flights of stairs. I learned many lessons from Mrs. Taylor about compassion and love.

We lived in the house with our grandparents, Ma-ma and Buddy. We listened to Ma-ma play the piano and sing praises to the Lord. We would join in on the songs as we played games not realizing that we were being touched by Ma-Ma's infectious faith. My great-grandmother and grandmother were both Sunday school teachers who taught us about God, His Son and how to pray. They prayed for us, and I knew that's why Jesus healed my heart. My mother and my biological dad were divorced when I was seven years old and his absence would leave a void in my life.

My aunt and cousins moved to their new house while Shelly, Jerry and I stayed with our Mom, Ma-ma, Buddy and Grandma, who was Ma-ma's mother. Grandma worked as a cook for a family at their house. She was only home on Wednesday's and Sunday's when she went to church. Buddy owned a seafood restaurant that closed late at night. Shelly, Jerry and I would climb in the bed with Ma-ma. We were only allowed to watch inspiring or comedy shows on the television, and Ma-ma would watch with us.

During my heart surgery doctors discovered that my spine was curved both outward and to the side. The diagnoses was (Kypho-scoliosis), I had a hump back. I was sent to Memorial Hospital, and then referred to Lutheran Hospital. The plan was to straighten my back. A plaster cast was molded of my back, and a Milwaukee brace was made of metal and leather. It was thought the brace would straighten the deformity in my back. I had to wear my clothes larger to fit over the brace, and I had to wear a retainer on my teeth, because the chin pad on the brace could allow my teeth to buck in an outward position. My schoolmates stared and I had to explain the brace time after time. They had never seen that kind of brace before, and neither had I until I had to wear one. My appointments with the doctor's were frequent, and I still could not jump rope or do anything strenuous.

Our mother worked during the day so we spent more time with Ma-ma who taught us to cut out shorts and skirts from a pattern. She taught us to sew on the sewing machine, and at twelve years old we could make a basic pair of shorts or a skirt. She taught us to cook, bake and clean. Ma-ma believed that if you want a child to learn something they must be taught, not just told how to do it. She had a God given gift to teach. Shelly, Jerry and I had chores, but we had awesome playtimes too. We collected empty cartons, boxes and containers. We cut up paper for money and had a store. We put dining room chairs together, two in front two in the back, and made a car. We used our imaginations and sometimes even Ma-ma's to go anywhere and to do anything.

When my granddad Buddy left the house for what he called the shop (his restaurant), Shelly, Jerry and I use to wait until he got down to the mailbox to start calling to him, "Buddy, Buddy!" He knew what we wanted and we started running towards him and he dug deep in his pocket and gave us each a nickel. "Thank you!" and we started running to the store and bought two for a penny candy. One day Buddy had to go into the hospital, Ma-ma and my mom went to see him. Then one night the phone rang and the doctor told Ma-ma to come to the hospital. Buddy had died from cancer.

Then I became a teenager, the only time in my life I felt like I knew it all. If I could only count the number of times that I told Ma-Ma and my mom, "You just don't understand!" As a teenager I enjoyed reading, I liked school and spending time with friends and family. I fell in love with words, whether reading or in music. Junior high school opened new doors for learning, friendships and yes, boys. Well one boy in particular who would be my friend for my entire teenage years. I disregarded my mother's, and Ma-ma's warnings of trouble; and I found myself in the very situation that I was warned about. My mother and Ma-ma were very disappointed in me. *Yeah, I thought I knew it all.* If I really did know it all, why didn't I know that this would happen? Why didn't I know that just as Ma-ma and my Mom predicted my friend of four years would be gone because I was going to have a baby? My doctor was concerned for my heart and other medical problems and I was in the high risk bracket, it was only by the grace of God that I delivered a healthy baby without complications. I had problems afterwards, which diminished my chances of having other children.

My mother married Rick and soon after we moved to Aberdeen Proving Ground where he was stationed in the army. I moved into a townhouse just off of the Proving Ground, but in walking distance of my parents home. Shelly and I rode bicycles together, and played ball with my little one and her friends in the yard. Shelly and I walked everywhere.

I loved to dance, and we danced wherever and whenever we could. I won dance contests and believed that dancing was a gift from God, the only gift that I was aware of. Sometimes as we walked I noticed weakness in my legs. While sitting my legs would jump with uncontrollable spasms. Dr. Davis recommended that I see an orthopedic surgeon. I met with Dr. Johnson, and after tests he explained to me that because of the curvature in my spine; I was losing the function of my legs. I was destined to be paralyzed because of pressure on my spinal cord. This could possibly be relieved with surgery, and may even restore normal leg function. There was concern for my heart, and many tests were done to assure its strength for the surgery. I prayed hard and I remember being very nervous when Dr. Johnson came in around 9:30 in the evening to talk with me about the surgery. My student nurse, Hailey, came in with a sign for me which read:

Faith is not merely,
you holding on to God;

it is God holding on to you,
He will not let you go!

After surgery Dr. Johnson told me that my spinal cord was only
partially decompressed. We would have to wait to see the results.
I was moved to a room from ICU the following week. I lay in my
bed staring out of the window of my room and I saw the biggest,
whitest, fluffiest cloud I had ever seen in my life. My heart was filled
with grief as I realized I had taken everything God had given me for
granted. I went to surgery praying that it would be a success, but the
worst thing that could have happened, happened—I was paralyzed.
Twenty-one years old and I couldn't dance, walk or do anything for
myself. I needed someone to turn me over and to give me a bath. I
had to be held in a sitting position because I had no muscles to hold
me. Numbness took over my sensation from the waist down. Imagine knowing that you have legs—you can see them and feel them
with your hands—but except for physically being there, your limbs
do not exist. I knew there was a reason for this, but what could it
be? I began to write poems, short stories and children's stories. I had
never written a word before I became paralyzed and now I wonder
if I could. Because of my medical problems and to express my level
of pain, I learned to pay great attention to detail. Is it a dull pain or
a stabbing pain? Does the pain stay in one place and if not does it
shoot down or does it radiate? I learned to be tuned in to my own
body for medical reasons.

Eventually I was taught basics in dressing myself. I was given
tools to pull on my socks, and my pants. I was taught to use a long
handled shoe horn to get my shoes on. My family spent Christmas
and New Years in the hospital with me. After a month long stay I
was released to go home by ambulance. Dr. Johnson ordered a hospital bed and a nurse for a few hours a day. My family would have to
fully take care of me. I wore a plaster body cast that began under my
arms and continued down to my hips. My new life truly hit me the
day I came home. I had to be bathed and dressed everyday, and sat
in my wheelchair where pillows were placed on either side to keep
me from falling to one side or the other. I was on a waiting list to
enter City Hospital for intense rehabilitation.

Finally the call came in April for admission into a year long program. That's where I met Jean, my roommate, who came in the next day. She had been in an accident and was paralyzed from the neck down. I immediately thanked God for my upper body strength. Ma-ma always said that there are people worse off than you are, no matter who you are or what you're going through.

In talking to Jean I found that she did not believe in God. I began to help her to do things that she could not do for herself. This was a huge blessing for me because taking care of someone else helped me to not dwell on myself. I learned to place my wheelchair behind Jean's and pushed her to, and from physical therapy. We used my upper body strength to even manage the elevators. We also enjoyed going outside on hospital property, which had wheelchair trails. I was so thankful that I knew and loved the Lord. I'm glad that I knew to praise Him in every situation good or bad. I would share with Jean all the Lord had done for me. I told her that He would do the same for her if she would talk to Him. Ma-ma said to "plant a seed and that God would open the heart."

In June my plaster cast was cut off and a plastic molded cast was conformed to my body. This was very different from the Milwaukee brace from years ago. This was not to straighten, but to keep me in the correct posture for the continued healing of my spine. This one allowed me to unfasten the Velcro closures to separate the front from the back. It was so much more comfortable than the plaster cast. This entire year was filled with therapy and blessings. I continued to plant seeds of the awesome power of God, and He provided proof of His power. As we concluded our year at the hospital, Jean was walking with crutches with arm supports up to her elbow. I was able to use crutches with my arms as my legs. I would lift my own body weight by using the mid crutch support. Although difficult, I could swing both of my legs forward. I would use my right leg which had just enough strength to stand for a second while I brought my crutches forward, but there was still no feeling from the waist down. I also used a prosthetic (leg brace) because I didn't have movement in my left ankle at all, and my left foot dangled below my ankle as if there were nothing but skin holding it to my leg. The leg brace was to hold my foot in an upward position. This would allow me to move forward for short distances without scraping my toes on the floor. I had to wear orthopedic shoes, ones that my brace could fit into. My shoes had to be a size larger. Even so, God is good and even Jean couldn't deny that.

After my release I had another year of physical therapy at home, which helped me to be a little more independent. I could move around in my wheelchair, but I missed walking, dancing and riding a bicycle. I sought leg strengthening exercises every chance that I could. However, I was advised that the longer I went without movement the less of a chance of my ever walking again. While still dealing with health issues I still struggled to live my everyday life with paralysis. Learning to cook, clean, and train my mind to do it all from my wheelchair.

I enrolled in a Rehabilitation School where I would have to be responsible for my daily appointments, classes and homework. This was a live-in school where I would have to live with a roommate. Here is where I witnessed God using limitations to His glory. My roommate, Carla, was blind, but more sighted than some seeing people. She was an inspiration to many of us. I obtained my G.E.D., and took classes in typing and clerical record keeping. I witnessed some who hid behind their own self pity, and therefore could not achieve their goals. I've learned that a positive attitude is vital to overcome any hurdle. I was forced to stop classes several times because of illness, but I always returned.

As I completed the Rehabilitation Center, I noticed that I became more fatigued than usual. I was running a rather high temperature. After tests, Dr. Rolland gave me antibiotics to treat a urinary tract infection. He encouraged me to rest until all of the blood work and throat culture results came in. At the end of the ten day dosage of the antibiotics my temperature spiked again. When antibiotics were not working to cure me my doctors began to look closer.

It was then that I was diagnosed with Bacterial Endocarditis (an infection in a valve in my heart). My doctors at the Military Medical Center began procedures to bring my step-dad, Rick, home from Korea. Blood cultures were taken a few times everyday that I was in the hospital. This was difficult for me because my veins were very tiny and I had to be stuck numerous times before they could actually draw blood. The first choice for an antibiotic to fight the infection was Vancomycin which drew an allergic reaction. I was treated for the reaction and then prescribed a different antibiotic. Since this infection had to be fought with a full six weeks of antibiotic therapy, I would be an inpatient at the hospital for that time. Doctor's advised that I be given penicillin before any minor surgery to prevent bacteria from entering into my body as this infection damaged the tricuspid valve on my heart. During this stay I began physical therapy for leg strengthening. Due to the ongoing paralysis in my lower extremities, my right leg was always bent under the weight of my body. My left leg would drag behind me, and I still had no sensation from the waist down. Although it was very unstable, it worked for very short distances.

I began to look for work using the skills I had acquired at the Rehabilitation Center. I moved into Ma-ma's house with her and grandma. I found work as a telephone operator by day, and banking at night. I caught a cab to and from work for a few years. I finally had to give up both positions for health reasons.

While flipping the remote one night I rested on a channel where a man looked into the camera and said, "Don't touch that dial." He asked his viewers to pray with him. I prayed the sinner's prayer accepting the Lord Jesus Christ as my personal Savior. I had always believed and depended on Him, but I had not surrendered my life to Him.

There was something different about this time. For years I studied the Bible from my bedroom at Ma-ma's house. I prayed for His Holy Spirit to dwell within me. I prayed for the scriptures to be magnified that I may understand, I fasted and meditated. "But the anointing which you have received from Him abides in you, and you do not need that anyone teach you; but as the same anointing teaches you concerning all things, and is true, and is not a lie, and just as it has taught you, you will abide in Him." (1 John 2:27) Day after day I was led through scriptures as the Holy Spirit disciplined and taught me, I was tested as God strengthened me for my continued journey. Only He knew that the roads were about to toughen.

I remember when grandma who was the queen of our lives told me that she was going upstairs. She was still very independent

     CONSUELLA CANADA

at ninety-five years old. I walked with her to the stairs and then I walked to the front door. I heard her walking back and forward in the hallway. I yelled up to her, and she told me that she couldn't find her way back to the steps. My heart sank to the floor as I used my crutches to help me to get upstairs. The most humble and honorable woman that I've ever known had slipped into old age and needed someone to help to care for her. A few family members came down to help, and we took turns sitting up with her through the night. When she was alert, I wrote down stories from her childhood, names of her ancestors and stories about her marriage. Grandma Rosa died after a long illness at ninety-nine years old. She left her strength, humbleness and faith as a lasting memorial of her relationship with Christ.

From the time of my open heart surgery my heart skipped beats, which meant it would beat slower. When I was younger it wasn't a concern but that changed as I had gotten older. This condition is called Bradycardia. This caused an insufficient oxygen supply to my brain, and caused me to feel lightheaded. Dr. Sans and Dr. Wilson inserted a dual chamber pacemaker into my chest to regulate my heart beat. The pacemaker was very uncomfortable at first because it was foreign to my body. I was assured that in the near future I wouldn't be able to tell that it was there. A technician continues to call monthly to test my pacemaker over the telephone, and I continue go to the hospital every six months for a thorough check. Finally a year after the surgery I noticed the pacemaker's presence less and less. It was also during this time that I applied and became a single foster parent as I had always wanted to mentor, guide and help others.

It seemed as though when I would take one step forward, life made me take two steps backward. This time I was admitted into the hospital for pneumonia. I was diagnosed with congestive heart failure. Dr. Sans prescribed other heart medications to assist my heart in pumping more efficiently.

He referred me to Dr. Coleman, a Pulmonologist, and after many tests, I was diagnosed with restrictive lung disease (because my lungs can not fully inflate due to my back and spine problems ,along with asthma), and also with obstructive lung disease (because

I had developed asthma, which limits the amount of air that I can take in and let out of my lungs). I began treatment by using a nebulizer to deliver medications to my lungs, and oxygen at night and during the day in high humidity. I continued to study, and I prayed to be worthy to be used by God, and my deepest prayer was for Christ like character.

Because of excruciating upper and lower back pain stemming from my Kypho-scoliosis. There were several years when I was completely confined to my bed. Walking to the bathroom was very hard because of pain, and a commode was positioned next to my bed. My life was filled with pain and I prayed for relief but mostly I continued to talk to God and asked for His strength and guidance. Although I had pain medication my stomach was very sensitive to many medications and often I had to choose between pain and nausea.

I was referred to a Rheumatologist to pinpoint the cause of the pain and he began testing. During these years of immobility, and the lack of exercise; my bones, tendons, muscles and joints have weakened. A bone density test, a bone scan and X-rays rendered a diagnosis of, rheumatoid arthritis, osteoponea, and osteo-arthritis. I also have degenerative discs disease in my spine (where the cushioning between my discs is deteriorating and my discs have collapsed on top of one another), and severe osteoporosis over my entire body, and because of my young age of forty-four there was much concern. My bone mass was compared to that of an eighty year old. I get fractures in my spine and hips called stress fractures from sitting or even sudden movement. It's very difficult to sit for long periods of time, and in order to relieve pain I have to shift my weight from one side to the other often.

When Ma-ma came to visit we always talked and prayed before going to bed, and I would kiss her goodnight and pull the covers up around her. That morning when we woke we heard the news of Princess Diana's death, and we talked about the tragedy. We prayed for the princess and her family. Ma-ma used that opportunity to tell me that she didn't want me to be upset if something would happen to her. She told me that it would make her sad if she knew that I was hurting. She also reminded me that Jesus would take care of her and not to worry. My husband served us breakfast upstairs as he did most of the time, and Ma-Ma always found something to say about being served that connected to how we are to serve Jesus.

A few years later my pacemaker had to be replaced. Shelly and Lisa went to the hospital with me. Great care was taken because of my previous heart problems and to avoid infection. When I woke I heard Shelly talking with the nurse and it was decided that I would stay over night for observation and would be released in the morning.

A second spinal fusion was being discussed because I was still suffering from excruciating back pain. I was also experiencing incontinence and other symptoms. Dr. Darius wanted to relieve some of the pain that kept me immobile, and this surgery was to free my spinal cord from discs that were deteriorating in my spine. The doctors used discs from a donor and bone graph taken from my left hip which were fused together and stabilized with two screws at the base of my spine. After this surgery I had a brace which fit tightly like a corset and there was to be no bending or lifting. I wanted to be healthy and the more I went through the more I sought the Lord for comfort. After the surgery I received therapy at home for a couple of weeks. My home therapist, Donna, recommended a more intense physical therapy—an inpatient in a rehabilitation program. This therapy would be more than two to three times per week. I was admitted into a rehabilitation hospital a few months after my spine surgery where I had therapy three times a day and I was given the same tools that I had to help me get dressed that I had when I first became paralyzed.

After the two weeks ended my therapist at the hospital requested two additional weeks of therapy. I used my time between sessions to read and study the bible. The therapists were teaching me once again how to pull on my pants, because I wasn't supposed to bend at the waist at all. I was taught how to get in and out of a car using a sliding board. I also had a refresher course on getting in and out of the shower and how to maneuver in the kitchen with my wheelchair. I worked hard and at least tried to do anything that was asked of me, regardless of whether I thought I could do it or not. I knew that my body had to be challenged in order to gain strength. I walked short distances with crutches with my left leg still dragging and my leg brace, my arms still served as my legs. The day before I was to be discharged my cardiologist wrote orders for a transesophageal echocardiogram (trans-e-sof-a-ge-al echo-cardio gram), a test that is used to look at the back side of a heart. I was mildly sedated for this test. The doctor inserted a very small tube with a tiny camera on the end of it down into my esophagus to take pictures of the back side of my heart. When the testing was over I was taken back to my room. I heard my therapist call my name and asked if I felt like going to therapy. I don't remember answering her but I know I wanted to say, "No, not today." During the course of that day and the next, the day I was supposed to go home, I became ill and couldn't talk; my throat became swollen and very sore. Dr. Sans called for the results of a CT scan that showed I had developed pneumonia. He immediately stopped all fluids as I was weak, and having a difficult time breathing.

When Dr. Sans left the room my nurse, Tina, started oxygen and by this time I was shivering from fever and my fingernails had turned blue. Tina told me that I needed to take another test and that she would go with me to hold my hand. She placed a pulse oximeter (to measure the oxygen level in my blood) on my stretcher and took me to X-ray. She and a respiratory therapist moved me from the stretcher to the X-ray table. The doctor needed me to be in a tilted, upright position. Tina and the respiratory therapist held me because I couldn't stand on my own. My oxygen level was in the seventy percent range, which is very low. I could see the monitor myself as Dr. Daniels asked me to take big gulps of this mixture. The mixture was spilling out of the side of my esophagus, and I heard him say loudly, "Whoa, Whoa!" yelling for me to stop drinking. Right then, they placed me back on the stretcher and rolled me into the hallway. The respiratory therapist began a nebulizer treatment as another doctor standing beside me introduced himself as Dr. Frank. He explained that my esophagus had been torn while performing the Trans-esophageal Echocardiogram test the day before. He told me that he would come back to my room to talk with me. This was around 10:00 p.m. After I was settled in my room, Dr. Frank explained that my chest cavity and lungs were now filled with fluid and infection. He looked at me very seriously, and told me that I had approximately three hours to live. He asked if I wanted to call my family, but added that I needed to go to surgery before they got there or that I would die. This phone call completely stunned my family—after all I was only there for physical therapy and scheduled to be discharged on this day. I looked into Dr. Frank's eyes and told him, "God has given me children to raise, and there is no way that He would take me from them, I trust Him to keep me." As God placed this assurance in my heart, and as those words came from my mouth, strength welled up inside of me that I didn't have before then. "He gives power to the weak, And to those who have no might He increases strength." (Isaiah 40:29)

Dr. Frank was ready to begin the surgery, but I waited for my family to arrive from Aberdeen, which was forty-five minutes away, and my husband and my girls from Essex. Dr. Frank paced the floor, and as soon as my family walked in the door the doctor told them that we didn't have much time. "I must do this surgery," I told my husband. He asked me if I wanted to be transferred to another hospital. I did not, but the doctors dismissed that idea. As Dr. Frank spoke with my family, my nurse, Tina, packed my belongings into bags. My daughter's India and Lisa were crying as they rushed me down the hall on a stretcher to ICU. My mother, Rick and Charles walked together in shock; and Shelly walked quickly beside my stretcher as she held my hand. The doctor prepared us, saying that I would need feeding tubes and a colostomy bag. They didn't know if I would ever talk again, that would determine on the extent of damage to my esophagus. I would be on life support indefinitely and possibly for life. Dr. Frank gave me a ten to twenty percent chance of survival, and said that I would require long term care in a rehabilitation hospital. Even after wounds healed, I would still have to be taught to walk, talk, and function, he added that my family would have to learn to tube feed and to care for me as I would be in a vegetated state.

I was given immediate care as soon as I reached ICU; and at almost the three hours predicted a call for the ERT (emergency rescue team) to ICU over and over as doctor's and nurses ran with a crash cart into my room. It took twenty-five minutes for the ERT to bring life back to my body. The doctors came out and talked to my family and they were told that I was in very critical condition, and that I had gone into complete cardiac and respiratory arrest, requiring resuscitation as my heart had stopped twice. Though my condition, the surgeons thought they needed to do this surgery to clean my infected chest cavity and to drain lungs of infection and fluid. The team had already nasotracheally intubated me, (placing a tubing down my nose to my lungs to open airways to help me to breathe). My husband reluctantly agreed to the surgery; he said that he remembered my words, "I must do this surgery," On the way to surgery my stretcher was pushed out in the hall so that my family could see me. There was a respiratory therapist on my stretcher over me pumping air into my nose and mouth until I was in the operating room where I would be connected again to the ventilator. My family kept vigil in the waiting room praying as they held on to one another, and to God.

There were two separate surgeries; an incision was made to repair the tear in my esophagus but the surgeons couldn't find the hole because of the massive swelling in my neck. A tube was inserted in my neck to drain fluid and they were forced to close the site without repair. Then a separate surgery to open my chest cavity to drain fluid built up in the pleura (a thin tissue covering the lungs and lining the interior wall of the chest cavity). Two tubes were placed in my right lung and one in the left. God brought me through surgery and now I was diagnosed with ARDS, (Adult Respiratory Distress Syndrome), in which all functioning of my lungs stopped—they stiffened under trauma and infection. Soon after that diagnoses, the ICU team learned that I was septic as my own blood because of infection had become as poison running through all of my organs. My temperature reached 105 degrees. A ventilator breathed for me as my family moved into the hospital to be close. My mom was standing in my room when a doctor told her that they should be thinking about disconnecting the ventilator. India and Lisa were on an elevator when two doctors on the elevator wanted to know why my life was being prolonged. They didn't know that my children were on that elevator listening to their conversation. Days turned into weeks as my condition was listed as very critical, death hovered over me but only in this world.

I heard the most beautiful voices and I remember being told that I was in a realm called the Comfort Zone, and that I was to rest while my body was healing. The praises to God were continuous—they were above beautiful, glorious and magnificent; praises seemed to be coming from everything and everywhere. I remember the most beautiful and clear water that seemed to be glistening. My spirit was flooded with knowledge and wisdom at a rate of speed that I could not have comprehended in my natural state. I was saturated in the Holy Spirit times one billion, and illuminated in light, soft yet brilliant. I was taught all things, and all that was being instilled and etched upon my heart would be unmovable, unshakable and untouched by this world; it keeps me from worldly thinking. Simply, as many others I have been set apart, I know without doubt that I do not belong here, and I do not live as though I do. I live with a fear of God that anything I do will be done in His sight. I will not be a victim of His wrath and I live my life accordingly.

In the Comfort Zone there was such urgency for our children who are being targeted. We are to teach them how much God loves them, and to be their safe haven in this world of turmoil and confusion. They do not, and can not understand the real dangers of this world, but we as adults do know. It is known that powers of darkness will weaken them with tricks, video games, movies, literature, with friends and toys that are meant to quietly, and some boldly to steal their souls. They are our responsibility and we will be held accountable for them!

Imagine being in the core of love shielded by light, and immersed in the most ultimate peace. I knew I was safe, but the world doubted because they only knew what they could see—death hovering over me. I only knew what I could feel and hear in the Comfort Zone, which was overwhelming love and peace. This would be another lesson as I will never and can never live for approval in this world because of what I heard and felt in the Comfort Zone.

For five weeks there were no signs of even the slightest change in my condition, as evident of daily X-rays, EKG's and CT scans. A total of seven blood transfusions and every available antibiotic were used to no avail fighting the infection that now racked my body. My 105 pound body with my 4ft 11in frame now weighed 153 pounds due to fluid retention. Now a tracheotomy was performed (cutting into the windpipe to relieve obstruction). After six weeks of being in a coma finally Dr. Sans and Dr. Coleman made the only choice that was left for an antibiotic, Vancomycin. This same medication when given in the past for my heart valve infection had given me allergic reactions such as hives and a swollen tongue. It was the last resort. This same medication along with the results of the tracheotomy would be the turning point in my condition. The process of regaining consciousness was gradual and engineered by spiritual hosts.

Imagine again being in the Holy Spirit times one billion and with every peak of consciousness came a heightened feeling of heaviness and sorrow during this three or four day period of entering into my natural and sinful state. I was greeted by the sin of this world through a television that was kept on in my room all the time. Once I had completely regained consciousness I still felt as though I was illuminated by the light. My spirit was filled to capacity in God's love and empowered to live. One of my nurses placed a sign on the door to my ICU room that read, "God's Miracle." Dr. Coleman and Dr. Frank were pleased that I was awake but the look on their faces was both of disbelief and amazement. I could tell that they were apprehensive about my total recovery, and they wanted to take things very slow. I was still running a temperature and on a ventilator, a heart monitor, and I had to have blood gases done every six hours. Respiratory therapists stayed very close to my room to keep check on the ventilator. They also administered nebulizer treatments. Although I was somewhat awake, I slept a lot. I remember the first night they turned me over and discovered I had a decubitus (bedsore) from lying on my back for a solid six weeks and it was opened down to the bone, Dr. Coleman wrote orders that I was not to be placed on my back but propped up on either side. I was not a vegetable as predicted. I didn't have a colostomy bag or feeding tubes. I did have a trachea tube in my throat that kept me from speaking, and moving was very hard because my body had tubes and the tubing from the ventilator taped on my mouth to hold it in place. There were two central lines which are IVs with needles inserted into large veins in my chest, and antibiotics, blood and other medications hung on two separate IV poles filled to capacity. The second central line was being used to draw blood and this would eliminate constantly being stuck. There were stitches where the central lines were moved around while I was sleeping. Parts of my memory were missing, and although I was football fan I didn't recognize the game. There was a round disc on my wall with numbers on it and I was told that it was a clock and it tells the time of day or night. Charles held my hand tightly as he thanked God that I was awake. He told me with tears in his eyes that he now knew what pain and anguish truly meant. My God daddy cried at the foot of the bed as my husband moved to let him get closer. There were so many machines in my room that there was only a tiny space beside my bed.

During this time I couldn't communicate because I was still very weak and also the trachea tube I had in my throat had to have a piece added that would allow me to speak, if I could speak. I tried repeatedly to get someone to understand my weak shaking hand gestures, but no one could. I desperately wanted them to know that I loved them, and to know all that I had felt and heard in the Comfort Zone. I couldn't communicate at all and no one could hear me—they couldn't read my chafed and barely moving lips. My nurse brought me a clipboard and a pen, but because of weakness I couldn't close my fingers together enough to hold the pen, though we tried several times that week. I prayed and talked to God as I still felt His love and warm glow from the Comfort Zone. This was the longest week of my life and I felt trapped inside myself because I couldn't communicate. I learned valuable lessons of how it would be if I did not get my voice back. I became very sensitive towards stroke victims and others who loose their voice for any reason.

The following week I tried to hold a pen on Monday and again on Wednesday; I could barely hold on and in very shaky and barely legible letters I wrote, July the what? India told me that it was Thursday, August 20, I wrote, No! I believed it was the day after surgery. She told me that I'd been asleep since July 11, and after I wrote those few words the pen fell from my hands and I couldn't grip it again. Dr. Frank came in and removed one of my chest tubes and I was given an X-ray three times a day every day even during my sleeping. My heart rate was between 138 and 154 and my blood pressure was very low. Dr. Coleman came in and with motions I told him that I wanted to eat and to drink. He explained that they weren't sure if the tear in my esophagus was healed but first he would get the piece added on my trachea tube to see if I could talk and I shook my head okay. A few days later Dr. Coleman and the speech therapist came in at the same time she changed the trachea and with all my family standing around Dr. Coleman told me to say "hi." My mouth opened and nothing came out, I tried again and again and finally I heard myself say, "Hi." My Mom and Rick had tears in their eyes and I heard her say "Thank You God, thank You!"

After I was used to less sedating medication I asked Dr. Coleman if I could sit in a chair. He was more than happy for me to get out of the bed. Lifting me would take two people, one under my arms while another would lift my legs. They took extra care because I was still connected to the ventilator and other equipment. While I was being weaned from the ventilator I remained overly congested. I did not have the strength to cough or keep my airway free of fluid, and it had to be cleared by suction (a tube was inserted down into my trachea tube). This was done often to help keep my lungs as clear as possible. A test was done and it was still not clear if my esophagus was healed or not, but Dr. Coleman allowed me to drink water, and I drank gallons. This surprised all who knew me because I never liked drinking water, but now I couldn't get enough. Along with the fact that I needed to be hydrated there was something about this water that made a difference. A couple of days later he ordered a liquid diet that contained green food coloring in everything, to be able to see by x-ray if my esophagus was leaking fluid. After a few more days Dr. Coleman asked me why I wasn't eating. I didn't have a big appetite but this green food was not the most appetizing, and he felt comfortable at this time to order a soft diet. Italian ice became my food of choice although I was also partial to steamed carrots.

I begged to get out of intensive care but Dr. Coleman told me that I had to eat. I truly tried to eat but my stomach was so small that one fork full of food and I felt full. I was kept in ICU for a longer period of time to be completely weaned from the ventilator. I was transferred to the vent floor for precautionary reasons, and where I would be watched closely.

God's perfect plan for my life had truly come together. I realized that this life experience brought me to understand the unity of body, mind and spirit. God reached right where I was to make clear that this awesome unity was complete. I was too weak to hold a bible to study so I meditated and prayed as I began the journey of recovery. I was back in therapy with no movement in my legs and major weakness even in my upper body. I was sent back to my room several times because my oxygen level would drop below a safe level with exercise. Dr. Jamison asked a surgeon to look at my back for possible surgery on the bedsore that was still open to the bone. He pulled infected skin from my back as tears rolled down my face, a nurse held my hand as the doctor told me that surgery may be required. I prayed and prayed to God, "I just want to go home now." I have lost the function of the bottom half of my right lung and oxygen would be needed for life to aid in supplying enough to my organs. The right side of my torso where the surgery was performed is now hard to the touch. It feels as if someone is continuously grabbing a fist full of my right lung, it feels so tight when breathing. I was told that this is from scar tissue along with the trauma to my lungs because of the illness. Mrs. Camora, the social worker, made plans to have a stair lift installed in my home, to bring me up and down the stairs. The fire department was alerted that I was disabled and could not get out of my home without their assistance, in case of emergency. They came to my home and placed stickers on my windows that would remind them if they were ever called.

Because I had an open bedsore and was bedridden I had to have an air mattress that would fill and release air as to not have pressure on any one part of my body for a long period of time. Along with my oxygen I had to have a machine to read the oxygen level in my body. Everything possible was done to make my home safe for me. Our younger children struggled to understand how Mommy could be coming home one minute, and being so very sick that they were not allowed to see her because of a comatose state the next. Dr. Jamison made arrangements for me to be discharged on

September 21, 1998, and taken home by ambulance. I could not sit up yet and was still in a degree of pain and weakness, so car travel was not recommended. I was relieved to be leaving the hospital, I had not told anyone about the nightmares that kept me on the edge all of the time, and they were all the same. Someone was chasing me down the hallway of the hospital and they would always catch me and cut my throat. I was glad to be going home where I wouldn't have them anymore.

I lay on the stretcher feeling every single bump of the ambulance, and when they pulled up to my house my family was there to welcome me. The attendants propped me up on pillows and placed a sheet over me and left. I was discharged with help a few times a week a nurse, a nurses aid, physical therapist, an occupational therapist, an oxygen supplier, and a social worker. I was so glad to be home although the nightmares continued night after night and I would wake up horrified that someone was chasing me. Sometimes Charles would wake me up from the nightmare where I would be out of breath, crying and fearing that someone was in the house. I fought to stay awake in fear of a recurring dream. My days had segments that were filled with flashbacks, torment and tears.

I went back for follow up X-rays and when approaching the hospital I would cry at the sight of the signs with the hospital name. I became anxious and afraid that I wouldn't come back home; I learned to close my eyes when going to the hospital until I was inside. For six months after I was released I had to get x-rays as close attention was being kept on my progress. My lungs were still fragile and still contained fluid.

Our little ones were staying close, and now we understand that they were told that I was coming home the next day and it turned into three months. We had no idea how this affected them until I had to go to the doctors and they would cry because they thought I wouldn't come back home. We learned to prepare them in advance for my appointments. The shape of my bedroom window was the same as the window to the ICU room and I had flashbacks of hearing heart monitors. These memories would begin a feeling of despair and hopelessness in my mind and tears that couldn't be controlled. Every visit seemed harder than the first. I didn't understand this kind of bondage, and I prayed with no relief in sight.

After the sixty-three day coma my short term memory was lost, which sometimes frustrated me because I could loose my train of thought very easily. I was grateful to be alive, but there was still this feeling of hopelessness. Mrs. Camora told me that my symptoms were consistent with post traumatic stress disorder, which affects many people after going through a traumatic event in their lives. She helped me to pin point things that would bring on these feelings, she called them triggers—the beeping of the heart monitor, some TV shows, and going past the hospital where I was injured. I never let anything control my mind and no one understood. I didn't understand, as I turned to any and all information on PTSD. My symptoms were hallmark. I prayed for the Lord to be with me, and I know that He was, as I would endure years of mind torturing memories and fears. I gave God the glory for all victories in my life, and over my mind would be no different. Mrs. Camora would try to get counseling or some kind of intervention, but my insurance wouldn't support any that would come to the house and I was not mobile.

During my three month absence, my husband had taken pictures of the boys, so that I wouldn't miss their summer. They looked forward to taking the pictures and it gave them hope. My neighbors and the staff at my children's school gave my family support. We all knew that it would take time to heal from the trauma both mentally and physically. There was a constant struggle to fight my way back to health, which took years. I still had not reached the level of strength that I had before the injury to my esophagus, my heart and lung failure, pneumonia and the adult respiratory distress syndrome, all with on going paralysis. My family came in from Aberdeen every weekend to give Charles a much needed break.

Christmas 1998 was both filled with sadness and joy. Since leaving the hospital the nightmares stepped up and I couldn't get the beeping of a heart monitor out of my head. I cried for no apparent reason, and my despair caused it to appear as if I wasn't glad to be alive, but I long to feel that peace from the Comfort Zone. The more I prayed the worse things seemed to get. I couldn't function because of flashbacks, my mind was tormented, and I just wanted this to stop.

I knew that this was an all out attack and I was so used to handling all that came against me physically; that attacking my mind would be an obvious strategy because I had no experience in defending it. I felt helpless in what was waged against my mind and I knew that this was blatant and violent anger, fury even. My mind was being cluttered with thoughts and fear of something that Jesus had already been victorious over; my life and my death. Through my tears I cried and prayed to Him. I became a warrior in prayer to protect my mind, my children or anything that I was passionate about. I learned to go boldly before God's throne. It may have appeared I was not happy to be alive, but I constantly thanked God for sparing my life. A part of me didn't like this world anymore and never has evil been more magnified to me as it is now after experiencing the Comfort Zone.

During this same time there was a tremendous outpouring of love and support from neighbors and health care workers who adopted our family for Christmas. There were toys and gifts along with homemade cookies. As I continued to fight, I prayed endlessly to protect my mind from all that has come against it. I fought to keep mind over matter with this PTSD and the next few years were filled with continued torment and struggle.

It was on a Saturday night when Charles came into our bedroom. He asked me if I would be okay while he left the house to go to church the next morning. I told him that I would be fine here. I could not get up on my own but I knew that this was an answer to my prayers. Charles and one of our sons joined the congregation of St. Stephen's church. He brought a tape of the sermon home for me to hear; and the next Sunday he dressed me, and the remainder of my family joined the church.

After a year my pastor appointed me the president of the New Members Ministry. I remember during one of our meetings I asked some of the ministry members to help me fulfill my dream to kneel at the alter to pray. They helped me from my wheelchair and gathered around me, supporting my body in a kneeling position. Those ladies held me for a few minutes as I worshiped honored and praised

God. They helped me back into my wheelchair we all praised Him as we hugged one another and my dream was fulfilled.

I sat in the congregation of my church home looking around at all of the wisdom and knowledge of the elders. Many of them walked past my wheelchair and touch my shoulders, my hands, and my heart. When they spoke, I listened for their wisdom. They possess what is real, and tried in their relationships with Jesus, and that's where I struggle to be.

I was hospitalized because of pneumonia, which triggered my congestive heart failure, asthma, and COPD (chronic obstructive pulmonary disease). I was treated with a diuretic (medication to reduce fluid in the body) and nebulizer treatments (medication for my lungs). Being in the hospital again brought back memories and fear from the previous time I spent there. A week later I was discharged. A nurse was to admit me into the home nursing program, but after her examination she said that in her medical opinion I needed to be in the hospital. She made arrangements on that day for admission into a different hospital. They suspected something may be wrong with my heart. The next day they did a procedure called a heart catheterization, and I was told that I needed a second open heart surgery. The surgeon who would be the best man for this particular surgery was out of the country until the following week. They believed that the hole repaired in 1963 had reopened, and there was also possibly another opening that allowed blood to back up in the wrong direction, filling my lungs. In the meantime I was very weak and I slept most of the time. The following week the doctor returned, and my family and I met with him. Dr. Collins spoke honestly with us, and as he talked I could hardly keep my head up or my eyes open from weakness. He scheduled the surgery for the following week. He explained that there could be a complication because of my prior chest surgeries—my heart may be stuck to scar tissue and to my rib cage he warned that it could complicate the surgery.

The evening before surgery I sat in the window of my hospital room and stared at an office building under construction, which was also a part of the hospital. I prayed for God to be with me through the surgery, and because I felt just a little apprehensive I spent this time with the Lord.

My eyes fixed on a crane on that construction sight. In the dusk of the evening there was a pulley shaped like a giant red heart; I heard words that brought tears to my eyes: *I will give you a new heart.* The image of that giant, red, heart shaped pulley was strong and tough. I wondered why I had not noticed it before this moment. I was also told *This will be the last major obstacle;* I cried as I thanked God and I told everyone who would listen that I was going to have a new heart.

Before every surgery as I was being put under anesthesia, I recited the, "Yea though I walk, through the valley of the shadow of death, I will fear no evil for thou art with me, Thy rod and Thy staff they comfort me…" (Psalm 23)

During the surgery it was found that my heart was indeed stuck to scar tissue between it and my rib cage. This separation was very tedious and there was a great deal of bleeding. The doctors found that the hole that was repaired in the previous open heart surgery was opened slightly. However that wasn't what was causing my symptoms; my pulmonary vein was on the wrong side of my heart and now, as I got older, presented a problem to my lungs. I was told that this was present during the first open heart surgery in 1963, but there was no knowledge of how to repair it then. Dr. Collins moved the large vein to the other side of my heart and the surgery was a success. My stay in ICU was only one night, and before I was moved to the cardiac floor the chest tubes were removed. I was given two units of blood as I had lost a lot during surgery, and it took four days after the surgery for my incision to stop bleeding because of scar tissue. I was given another two units over the next few days. My arms continued to serve as my legs, and to move around would be to put stress on my rib cage, the incision and the wires that held my chest together. I was limited to my electric wheelchair because I could not roll myself around with the manual one. There was a lot of discomfort with strange beats and palpitations of my heart. They were very different from the normal feelings. It took about a year to regain my strength. A church member heard of my need for an adjustable bed because I needed to sleep in a sitting position. He offered me one for my recuperation.

This time was filled with pain from stress fractures that came from sitting because of my limitation to my wheelchair. I had to continue to shift my weight from one position to another to relieve pain. My rheumatologist sent me to the pain clinic that now manages my pain with medication. I have come to appreciate that our body's are God's temple and we should do all to maintain it.

Ma-ma came for a visit as she often did, and I used these opportunities to teach our sons to serve the elderly. We spend time together praying and sitting out on the porch. We laugh about things Shelly, Jerry and I used to do when we were little. She shared with me that teaching me to sew on the sewing machine, cutting from patterns, crocheting and knitting were all to keep me from running and jumping around. Mission accomplished.

After she is in bed I always go to her room to kiss and tell her that I love her. I turn off the lights and pull the door almost closed. I thanked God that I was able to give back a small portion of what she gave me, peace of mind. When we were told that Ma-ma had pancreatic cancer she has been given six months at best to live. She was ninety-two years old and though it hurts she has done her work for the Lord. She has been blessed with long life because of her service to the Lord, to her parents and to people. I didn't want her to leave me because no one else knew or understood me like she did. I know that I was being totally selfish, but I couldn't imagine my life without her. I prayed and asked God to give me strength. Ma-ma came to visit us a few more times, and when she couldn't come anymore we went to my mom's house to visit her. Just one month later my mother called and told me that they were taking Ma-Ma to the hospital. Ma-ma's body had begun to shut down we went to the hospital to be with her. I talked to her and rubbed her head and her hands. I went into the hallway and my cousin came and told me that Ma-ma wanted to see me. I went in and told her that I loved her; she was anxious and I couldn't understand what she was saying, but I knew what it was about. She was concerned about me. I told her that I would be okay and I kissed her cheek. We went back home while Shelly stayed at the hospital through the night.

The next day India and Lisa took me to the hospital. We stayed until visiting hours were over, and as we parked the car Charles told us that we needed to go back to the hospital. Ma-ma died and so did something inside of me. While I was grieving I thought that my heart would never heal, but it did with time. I missed her so very much, but she told me that she would not ever leave me, and I know that she hasn't. She lives inside my heart, and in the millions of memories alive in my head.

I awoke on a glorious Saturday morning in October 2002. In turning over I felt a spark of life in my lower body more specifically in my left leg. I heard the voice that I had become accustomed to instructing me, "Do not use your wheelchair for distances that you could maneuver," and "Do not use your stair lift," which I depended on to carry me up and down the stairs. I began to praise God because I know that He is a God of completion. He had begun a mighty work and my faith in Him would carry me through this process. My legs were very weak, and I was afraid. Even so, I was up walking on crutches that very same day. The next morning I was getting ready for church and as I praised God, tears streamed down my face. God was communicating directly with my spirit, which was accepting a steady and rapid flow of strength. My spirit was in complete agreement to God's will as I answered. "Yes Lord, Yes Lord," even though my physical body could not comprehend what I was agreeing to. There was such a calm that I could tell in my spirit when that experience was over that it was complete, it was solid, and it was done.

I walked from the bathroom to the bedroom on my crutches. My boys came in as I sat down on the bed. Tarrence asked if I could stand up, and although shaky I stood up and they said, "We want a stand-up hug like yesterday." This brought tears to my eyes. They appreciated stand-up hugs because they weren't use to their mom standing and those hugs were the door I used to tell them of God's miracles. Not just this one but the ones we've heard about on TV, and in the Bible.

My muscles began to constantly move with tiny little spasms that could be seen visibly, as if little tiny frogs were jumping in my leg. I understand that God could have touched me and my legs could have been miraculously restored. This too was a part of His perfect will for my life. God knew that I would understand and be accepting of how He chose to heal me. I know that He was using me, and this was an honor for me. Just as our life journey is a process so was this healing a perfected process, with God as the potter, and I as the clay.

I felt every change in my body, my spirit and also in my mind and heart. Years of falsely depending on my right leg brought the realization that what I truly depended on were my arms to hold me up. Physical therapy was recommended, but I declined as to have God do His work, in His time.

I remember walking to the front of the church with my crutches. I heard the applause of my church family as I stood before them. The last time I saw them I was in my wheelchair. Meanwhile I told everyone what God had been doing for me, and how once He gave this leg even the tiniest spark of life. He immediately opened a door that I should learn more about the mission of evangelism. In this class I learned to stand for devotions and prayer to open and to close out our classes. God used this time to train my knees and to strengthen my legs, and my faith while building my confidence. Although there were times that I felt as though I would fall. I silently prayed for strength. The first few weeks of class were eye opening. The hymn "Blessed Assurance" became more than wonderful words to me. This truly is my story, and it is my song. God had already set me in the perfect position in my church home where I encouraged our new members. Our assignment was to spread the good news of the Christ; these evangelism classes taught me how to encourage others with the truth about Christ. It taught me about sin and eternal life. It took what I already knew, clarified it, and then taught me to effectively share with others. God confirmed over and over again after seeing lives changed. This change was not just on the surface, but to the core of one's heart. This further humbled me after witnessing a change that would cause a lasting relationship with Christ. All that was needed was for the truth to be completely understood. *"And you shall know the truth, and the truth shall make you free." (John 8:32)*

There was a minor set back when I broke my toe but I didn't

allow that to break my will to do. Nor did I entertain any negative thoughts that may have over shadowed what God was doing for me, in me or through me. I continued to walk and to attend classes. I shared my testimony about the grace and mercy of our God wherever I went. He began to use me to minister to others. During the thirteen week course I shared with my class that God sent me there to build and to teach me to have the confidence and faith to complete His will for my life. Before this class I used to talk to people about Jesus, but now I know that confidence, and being sure of your own salvation is crucial in delivering to others. It will not have the same affect when your words are empty or without substance. God knows our hearts and we can not lead His people if He is not leading us. I found my passion, not in just speaking words, but bringing the truth to hearts that God will prepare. They will not only hear Him, but have a desire to obey His voice. As my class drew to a close I knew that God led me exactly to where I should be. I would be diligent in serving Him and Hearing what I am to do. There are many facets to our serving, and I will always ask His guidance for His people. I want to always be prepared to be used to His glory, this is who I am.

Still in the midst of healing after being paralyzed for twenty-seven years, I knew there was a reason why God had chosen this process of healing for me; although I couldn't comprehend it, He knew that I would be accepting to this process. Under my skin, my thigh muscles continued to dance with constant movement that filled me with the joy of the spirit and led me to tears and to worship God. I wanted to know what was going on the inside of my leg as I searched and found a picture of the muscle structure of the leg; I could not believe the awesome architecture that was before me. I could look at the picture and see what muscle was coming out of a solid and stiff state to function and how it is supported by other muscles, tendons, ligaments, and bone. That led me to remember the awesome creations of the Lord, and how every organ of our body is assisted by the other. How skillfully wrought is our physical body. I've learned that this is God's intention for His church, which is His body, our marriages which symbolize the relationship between

Christ and His church and our lives. All of it is to work in this same harmonious and divine order and all to the glory of God.

It became a habit for me to allow time for God that He could work with my spirit and my physical being. I needed to hear what I was to do and I needed to be in His presence. As this healing continued He used every tiny muscle spasm as a burst of spiritual strength. My spirit urged me to walk, and I learned quickly that when the spirit urged, I couldn't refuse. I began to walk one mile every day on my crutches and as I walked I could feel a hardened muscle begin to gently jump until it was movable; there were tears from being in a spiritual state of overflowing joy deep within my soul with each step I praised God.

Due to my history with paralysis I was very used to involuntary movements; but this was totally different. As I walked I could see and feel movements and muscles building. I encouraged people to watch closely because this was a miracle in progress. I kept asking if they saw changes in how I was walking, and often the answer was no. I couldn't understand why; I could feel and see the difference and though disappointed I remembered that this was my body and I couldn't expect anyone else to feel or see what I did. I used an odometer to show how far I walked in steps and in miles. It took an entire year for me to make a mental change to trust my legs even slightly. I saw my foot change from simply dangling from my ankle with a few threads keeping them together—my ankle felt different, like it had substance. There were ligaments and muscle holding my foot to my ankle and without my brace my foot would swing outward with my big toe grazing the floor because I couldn't lift it. My legs were holding very little of my weight although I felt I had begun to walk in a normal pattern.

It was on a Sunday while doing my walking, that in the middle of a lap I felt the bottom of my foot inside my shoe. This feeling was magnified because now I realized that I had not felt feeling in my foot before. My spirit rejoiced as tears rolled down my face. Through these twenty-seven years I lost the reality of sensation from my waist down, it had become normal not to feel and my mind eventually accepted this as normal. I realized that although I had some slight movement in my right leg before this, I had no sensation from the waist down. Now I could feel the bottom of my foot inside of my shoe as I walked. This was the most awesome feeling, yet it was a feeling I would have to get used to. I yelled for Charles to come inside of the house. I told him that I had sensation on the bottom of my foot.

One could visually see that my legs, which once looked as if skin was draped over bone, now had muscle mass building. I yelled to Charles as I held both hands up praising God. As another stage of this healing began, this one taught me to place the heel of my foot down before my toes. "All of these years I've simply placed my foot flat down because I had forgotten how to walk," I said with tears in my eyes.

Charles took some steps in front of me and then he turned and said, "You know your heel does go down first." He stood back and watched me take some steps as he shook his head.

"Yea, we take so much for granted." I added. This displayed the perfect planning of God. First I had to feel my foot in the bottom of my shoe in order to comprehend that my heel goes down first. I began to praise God for all He allowed me to see, to feel and to hear. He had my undivided attention as His Majesty led me through this healing. I learned how to make steps instead of swinging my leg forward, and putting my foot down.

After 37.95 miles, the routine was changed. Now I was not to focus completely on walking, but on leg lifting. During this time, while in a sitting position trying to lift my leg was like my 115 pound body lifting 110 pound weight for the first time. I exercised to music that lifted and praised the Lord. This helped keep me focused and only with His strength could I do this. I learned during this healing that it takes tremendous power to move our limbs. I know that if we each had to work for this power we would appreciate, and not take for granted, what our God has so graciously and freely given to us. This power is above our comprehension unless you've ever had to work for it. Only then will you understand how hard it is to gain that power back with your own strength once it is lost.

One Sunday morning I woke and told Charles that I was going to use my cane instead of my crutches for the first time. "Are you sure?" He asked. I was apprehensive and I didn't think my legs were strong enough. They had just begun accepting a little of my weight. My spirit urged my physical body to do it. For a fleeting moment I doubted and second guessed this decision, "No, I will do this," I said. I was afraid because I had never walked with a cane before, and my body was shaky and nervous. I had no confidence in this new independence. I did trust God and I felt very strong, yet I didn't trust my legs as I went before Him in prayer.

Father God, in You I place my trust. I've heard You and I will walk with this cane leaning completely on You. Even though I am afraid, I know that You will be my strength, and I thank You. In Jesus' name I pray. Amen. The scripture came to mind "My grace is sufficient for you, for My strength is made perfect in weakness," (2 Corinthians 12:9).

I picked up my cane and began to walk, I was nervous and I asked one of my children to walk beside me. I understood why the spirit led me to the cane. As long as I was still dependant on my arms and the crutches, my legs could not accept more weight and I had to let the crutches go to move ahead. Just as I had gotten up from that bed on that glorious Saturday morning, with new life in my legs though afraid, I was obedient to the voice of God.

My rheumatologist requested I go to physical therapy for my arthritis and joint pain. I had an evaluation on the first visit and the therapist was in awe that I walked with a cane because my legs did not have the strength to do most of the tests in the evaluation. While lying on my back, I could move my right leg out away from my body and back. My left leg was weak, and took an extra effort. I couldn't lie on my back and keep my knees bent with my feet flat on the mat. They would collapse outward. Lying on my stomach, I couldn't bend my legs up towards my back on either leg. After the exam on the mat, Cindy asked me to walk for her and she watched as I walked down about thirty feet and back. I saw her shaking her head as she said, "You're getting strength from somewhere."

"Yes, God is so awesome," I said.

She recommended that I take aqua therapy in a heated pool, and in this God given natural healer and cleanser I could move my legs freely as if I were one hundred percent healed. I could walk, do bicycle motions with my legs and even swim. I could not comprehend this, but my therapist explained that gravity does not hold you down in water. It creates a weightlessness much like an astronaut has in space. Because of the feeling of weightlessness, to my amazement, I could move freely. I began thinking about all that I was taught in the Comfort Zone about water as a natural healer. This therapy relieved my chronic pain and strengthened me. I noticed that once out of the water my limbs were so heavy that I could hardly walk. My therapist explained that because your limbs are so light you work harder although it may not seem like it. She said that my legs were very tired because of the exercise and the pull of gravity amplified this feeling. While I took water therapy a few times I had no pain. The miracle of water therapy is beyond belief. I was the youngest person as most were older patients. We all had a common goal—relief of joint pain. One day while I was in the water exercising, I pointed out to a therapist at the top of my leg where I was feeling a muscle that felt like a rubber band stretching. "Unbelievable," she looked at me and shook her head again.

I shared my testimony about my twenty-seven years of paralysis and others shared with me. That's the wonderful thing about testimonies; no matter how awesome yours is someone else's can inspire you because theirs is just as awesome. That's because the author of our lives brings us all to the same place where we can use all He's brought us through. Suffering and hurt have been transformed into blessings used to encourage, comfort and touch one another. So many people are going through and have been through the same and even worse ordeals than I. Make a conscious decision to exercise your faith in God and have the confidence in Him to show that you trust Him completely.

It has been two years since I felt that first spark in my leg. I've depended on what little strength I have in my right leg, and I'm not allowing my left leg to assist me. I'm still using my arms to lift me up from a sitting position; this is normal for me. I struggle to change my mindset by trying to remind myself to use my legs. When I became paralyzed I didn't have to struggle to learn not to move my limbs because I just couldn't. I do have to learn to use them again, and it's been very difficult. I sprained my right ankle, which forced me to depend on my left leg. Sometimes blessings come in unexpected ways—my ankle injury was painful, but it wasn't broken. It was during this time that I gained the most strength in my left leg.

In my trials and tribulations I have learned patience and obedience. I've learned how to truly walk with God from my wheelchair. I continue to ask him to change me and to guide me.

The plan God has for our lives can only be fulfilled in having a personal relationship with Him through Christ. I've learned that God uses our life experiences not only to strengthen us, but to bring family members, friends and all who may witness His power, to Him. He said: "This sickness is not unto death, but for the glory of God, that the Son of God may be glorified through it." (John 11:4) I've learned not to stress myself out on my trials and tribulations because God is there and inside of those situations, though you may not see Him. In His strength He will use you to make a doctor smile, to give a nurse comfort. Through you someone else may gain hope and strength as they watch you exercise your own faith in God. No matter how sick I appeared to be, God always gave me words of encouragement for others.

My legs are continuing to gain strength. I still stand in awe of the healing that is taking place inside of my body. After three consecutive times injuring my right ankle and foot, my left leg is strong enough now to take my total weight. It was the best possible solution to the problem. I am beginning to use my legs to lift me from a sitting position. I am able to feel the muscles in my feet moving, although there's still an extra effort and my toes are still hard to move. I still walk with a cane and now my legs are holding my total weight. Soon I will lay this leg brace down for the last time. Inside of my house I'm taking steps without the cane and I am humbled in just the thought of our faithful and awesome God.

The Lord knows what we are going through, because He's been there. He is with you, and will be on the other end of the storm waiting for you with His arms out stretched to celebrate the victory with you. Every illness, struggle, pain and suffering, all of it brings us into closer fellowship with Christ. I wouldn't change one day of my life, and I am thankful I have learned that God is worthy to be praised. He is worthy of our obedience and our loyalty. He will never ask us to do anything that He has not already done for us—all the way to death. He is faithful to reward us with the fruit of the spirit—Christ like character. Although we may go through some things, nothing that we could ever go through will match what Jesus has already gone through for us.

We must look through our trials and tribulations so that we may reap the benefits God has already ordained for our lives. All that we go through is to urge us to talk to Him, to trust in Him. He loves us and everything that He has brought me through, He will also bring any of His children through. It is not because I'm special or even that I have a special work to do for Him, because in God's sight we're all special and we all have a special work to do. It's because I diligently seek Him. I thirst for His wisdom, and I long to be Christ like. In my journey God has been nothing but faithful to me, and I have chosen to be faithful to Him. My journey continues as God begins to teach me about His love, and relationships.

The Darkness before Dawn

I can't comprehend how you've all managed,
as you hearts and your lives were suddenly damaged.
Both day and night while you all stood by my bed,
it may have seemed hopeless, but our souls were being led.
I gained strength from each stroke of your loving hands,
and from each tiny mention of our future plans.
As I was escorted back to you,
I was told that my life had been renewed.
Every one of your prayers for God's will to be done,
brought us all closer to His only Son.
Let us not forget when the hurt and pain subsides,
that there could not have been a miracle
without Jesus as our guide.

My Lord, My God

My Lord, my God, how great you are,
You have been my strength right from the start.
You've lifted my spirit when my heart was down,
You lifted me to a much higher ground.
My Lord, my God, my beam of light,

Guide my days and light my nights.
I vow to walk in steadfast faith,
My Lord, my God, please keep me safe.

RELATIONSHIPS

Relationships are important, and they all begin with God and Jesus—with Adam and Eve, and when He created us for Himself, and each other.

Before I was saved, most of my relationships were riddled with jealousy, envy, lies and gossip. I used my tongue to slander, lie, and to use some of the vilest language known. That was how I talked and everyone who knew me knew it, and that was expected of me. This was one of the toughest lessons of all. It took years for me to learn to control my tongue.

As I watched television in my bedroom at my grandmother's house, I flicked through the channels, when I heard a voice saying, *Don't change that channel,* I joined with a man in repeating the sinners prayer, and accepted Jesus Christ as my personal Savior. I had done this before, but this time was different. I thirsted for the word of God. I prayed for Him to strengthen me, and I became a willing participant in this relationship. I made a choice to study, pray and to seek God, everyday. My choice became the door which God used to manifest Himself. "Behold, I stand at the door and knock, if anyone hears My voice and opens the door, I will come in to him and dine with him and he with Me," (Revelation 3:20).

Prayer is a vital part of this relationship—we must pray, praise, and worship God throughout our day, everyday. We can easily get caught up by diversions in life. Televisions, video games, telephones and computers—all of them can take time from our relationship with the Lord. By allowing these things to distract us we become willing participants in the sins of omission. These are the things that we're suppose to do, but do not do them for one reason, or another—studying, reading the bible, praying or going to church are just some examples.

I can get so caught up on my computer from morning to night, especially if I'm researching. I had to limit my work habits, my computer time, and everything that monopolized my time which is now so valuable to me. I've done some little things that help my relationship with Him. I've attached praises to the Lord to some of the things I do daily. I've fixed it so that it's impossible to do them without that praise. Because I treasure the time in fellowship with the Lord, I pray Psalm 51 to cleanse my mind and my heart because I want to be worthy to spend this time with Him, after all He is my Lord.

I pray for understanding and wisdom, and the Holy Spirit ministered to my heart through the book of Proverbs. I needed to learn what was expected of me in this relationship, and I studied the letters and teachings of Paul. I have been comforted in prayer, and ministered to through meditation. I am strengthened through trials and tribulations. I've learned to follow the Lord's lead through scripture, as I was being taught how to totally trust in Him. I've learned to keep things within reach to keep me focused: the Bible or something inspirational to read, a prayer on my lips, and a constant I thank you. I could see the difference in handling a situation myself, and when I allowed Jesus to work it out. I struggled as the Holy Spirit guided me through some very tough lessons. My way of thinking was being altered, and at the same time I had to cope with one life experience after another. "And do not be conformed to this world, but be transformed by the renewing of your mind, that you may prove what is that good and acceptable and perfect will of God." (Romans 12:2)

Along with worship, prayer and praise we must learn to trust, and have faith. I was forced by the circumstances in my life to trust in the Lord, the more trials the more stable my faith in Him became. This intimate relationship became stronger, and before I realized it fifteen years had gone by. I studied and prayed to be as much like Jesus as humanly possible. I allowed change as I worked hard to change. With every victory, no matter how small, I praised the Lord. Even as this relationship was growing, it took years for me to learn to control my tongue. I prayed, and as I trusted in the Lord, the Holy Spirit led me to the third chapter of James. Here I learned the deceitfulness of my tongue. I prayed for God to "Let the words of my mouth and the meditation of my heart be acceptable in Your sight, O Lord, my strength and my Redeemer," (Psalm 19:14). This lesson is ongoing. The Lord has placed words in my heart to encourage and comfort and I see the changes. My relationship with the Lord led me to have a more quiet and humbled spirit and I guard my words, and they are few unless I'm teaching or praying. I've learned to pray and be patient while waiting on the Lord in times of trouble. Since my experience in the Comfort Zone I pray, and I worship Him, and then I listen for His voice. I access His peace through prayer which has become an even larger part of my everyday life.

My relationship with Jesus is my safe haven; He came to the door of death to rescue me, and sheltered me in the Comfort Zone. I became so comfortable with Him that no matter what I may go through even when death is over me, I will trust in God. I rested on Jesus and on the promises God. Jesus promised, "I will not leave you nor forsake you." (Hebrews 13:5a).

It was there I learned the value of true love; it is not a feeling or an emotion. God began this next lesson on the inside of my very own heart. Love is the act of placing others before you, it's sacrificing yourself. That's what God did when He sent His only Son to die for us, and that's what Jesus did when He died on the cross for humanity. We must sacrifice the way we want to live for how God wants us to live. When we do that the love in us is made perfect, and we begin to see others through God's eyes, discernment included. First I had to learn to love myself, and after I understood that I was fearfully and wonderfully made, that He made the days for me not me for the days (Psalm 139); that God Himself breathed the breath of life in me (Genesis 2:7); when I comprehended that even before I was formed in the womb God knew me, and ordained me to do a work for Him; (Jeremiah 1:5); only after I realized how much He loved me did I begin to see my value through His eyes. This knowledge shed light on the value of each and every one of us. It caused me to treat others respectfully, and I stopped searching for someone to validate me. God did that when He breathed life into me, and Jesus confirmed who I was when he died for me. When I accepted these truths all voids in my life were filled. No longer did I look at the faults of others, I focused more on correcting my own behavior, and on my own personal relationship with the Lord. When I began to use this new wisdom my relationships with others blossomed.

Some of us are using hurt and pain as a shield to keep love at bay, but true love from God will break down all bearers. "Hatred stirs up strife, but love covers all sins." (Proverbs 10:12) True love blanketed my life and I used what I'd learned, and it positively impacted my life. As the next life experience was laid before me.

A very young lady who spent a lot of time with our family stayed with us for a while, and in sharing with Loren, God touched my love for children. Her visit inspired me to reach beyond my own, and this would begin a journey that I could have only taken by the grace of God. I remember coming from a doctor's appointment and seeing the inner city street corners filled with young men and women. I said to a friend how I wished I could make a difference in the younger generation. It was during this time that the larger purpose of God's sending Loren to us came into focus. This led me to the Foster Care system, and God was ready for me to extend my gifts to touch others. Many of us had inherited Ma-ma's natural ability to teach. God's plan had just begun as I became a single foster parent at thirty-two to an eight month old; no child came without prayer and no child left without prayer. I planted a seed of love that the babies may not remember, but I trust God who sent them to me and He will keep His hands on them. After several children I adopted as a single parent, amidst the predictions from the agency that I wouldn't qualify due to my health issues. I was able to give my son what God had given me, unconditional love. Because of lessons learned I understood how important we are to one another. It has nothing to do with skin color, and everything to do with our relationship with Jesus. Warfare is real, and we need the support of other Christians, in fellowship, prayer and encouragement. My relationship with others is firmly grounded in real and complete love from God. There is nothing more precious than His love, which is spiritual. After experiencing His love I'm not easily impressed with anything that doesn't involve Him, but I am impressed when we share His love with one another.

We have partially destroyed our relationships with one another because of our sinfulness in fornication, adultery, and substance abuse. We have helped to destroy the family, but God is the ultimate Family Maker. He places people together to build families; sometimes blood connects them, and others are connected by love. God has blessed us with children who grew inside of our hearts, which He had already prepared for this birth. As He sent another child to me for adoption it became very clear that God's love is the most important element in family. It's a bond that blood doesn't naturally give you. As I learned these lessons, I understood that we must go through the same process when becoming children of God. When we accept Jesus as our personal Savior we become a part of God's family. "For you did not receive the spirit of bondage again to fear, but you received the Spirit of adoption by whom we cry out 'Abba, Father.'" (Romans 8:15) We are adopted by God through Jesus, and this relationship is all about spirit and love because our Father is both.

God has placed people in our paths, some are here to teach us compassion, some to encourage us, but all relationships can teach us something to help us to grow. Because of my grandmother's relationship with the Lord she recognized who I am in Him. God allowed her to see me through His eyes; I didn't have to pretend, or to be on guard with her. Ma-ma knew me, and she is the reason I strived to know my true identity in the Lord. God placed her in my life and I nursed on her wisdom and courage. She shared, guided and encouraged me to find Him, and I was receptive to her teaching. Our family's bond became stronger with time and this bond would be tested and strengthened as we learned lessons in loyalty. Our relationships in families as well as Christians should be as loyal as Naomi was to Ruth (Ruth 1).

> "Therefore if there is any consolation in Christ, if any comfort of love, if any fellowship of the Spirit, if any affection and mercy, fulfill my joy by being likeminded, have the same love, being of one accord, of one mind. Let nothing be done through selfish ambition or conceit, but in lowliness of mind let each esteem others better than himself. Let each of you look out not only for his own interests, but also for the interests of others. (Philippians 2:1–4)

God created us to make contributions to the lives of others through His love which can conquer all. His love is the love expressed in (1 Corinthians 13), and is beyond our comprehension until we are saturated with it. There is no greater love than from God because He is love. His love was shown in His sacrifice for us. Our relationship with God can only be filled through Jesus Christ and its rewards are many and they are eternal. In the power of true love all relationships will mature and grow. We should not take this word "love," for granted, nor take it lightly; true love is power from God our Father. It is the true essence of God. This love will not only show on our faces but in our actions and from our mouths. Others will be able to feel it, and to see it. Jesus' love for each of His disciples was individual, yet He loved them collectively. He holds that same love for us, individually yet as one. Each one of the disciples brought a different dimension to Jesus' ministry as a whole, and it's the same in our lives. Each relationship should be treated individually and according to the needs of that particular person. Our love should be evident for people as a whole.

While still more trials and tribulations surrounded me, God strengthened my love and continued to build my character. As our relationship with God is being nurtured, fed and maintained, He will be equipping us to do His work. God will use you right where you are in your relationship with Him. You don't have to know every scripture in the Bible, or every ritual held in the church.

My Comfort Zone experience has heightened my sense of responsibility for our children. We must not only pray, but be relentless in teaching, encouraging, and helping them to be sure of their own salvation. We must help them to recognize their own spiritual gifts, and begin to use them to serve the Lord and others. We must lead them to God by helping them to strengthen their personal relationships with Jesus. We must teach them the only truth that will set them free, the Word of God. We must teach them the nature of God and His power, teaching them how He will take care of us, just as He did with the children of Israel while in the wilderness. He fed them bread from heaven, (Exodus 16:15–18). They need to know how He gave Abraham and Sarah a child, although they were both very old, (Genesis 18:11–18). Our children must truly know God, and to fear Him as we all should. But also to know how much He loves them that they will serve Him and honor Him.

We don't give our children the credit they deserve. We have above-average young people today. If children can be taught to hate others simply because they live in another country, so much that they will strap a bomb to their bodies, and kill themselves in order to kill the citizens of that country, I ask you, how much good could children do in learning, knowing and possessing God's love in them for the saving of mankind? As Christians they should see the power of God in us and I guarantee that it would make a difference in their lives. When we have a relationship with God and when He lives in us, others will be drawn to Him in us. "And I, if I am lifted up from the earth, will draw all peoples to myself," (John 12:32).

When we have a relationship with God through Jesus He shines in us and others may not know what it is, but there is this little something about you. It may well be that they're being drawn to you, because the Lord is shining through you. Your relationship with Christ is the foundation for all other relationships. Now that I am rooted and grounded in Him, He has prepared me to share my life with someone else.

Change Me

Change my ways, and keep me strong,
Clear my mind from all that's wrong
Help me choose my words just right,
Keep me always in Your light.

"And do not be conformed to this world, but be transformed by the renewing of your mind, that you may prove what is that good and acceptable and perfect will of God." (Romans 12:2)

I Know a Friend

I know a friend who will do whatever we asked Him to;
He will heal our bodies, save our souls, whatever we ask He'll do.
He'll lift our spirits and feed us words for us to share with friends.
He'll give us peace and love and our aching hearts will mend.

Call on His name and He'll be there to love and to teach us.
Give thanks to God for sending us a friend called Christ Jesus.

MARRIAGE

AT LAST MY WEDDING DAY. IT TOOK THIRTY-SEVEN YEARS OF my life, to evolve into the person who was ready to commit her whole life to another human being. I fully understood that my vows were both to my husband and to God, and that they were meant to last forever.

I remember a sleepless night, anxiously awaiting the sunrise on this day that we'd been preparing for. Charles and I were raised in the same neighborhood, and have been friends since I was seven years old. We played together, walked to elementary school together, played in one another's homes and our families were acquainted. This will be Charles' second marriage; the first gave him two children. This would be my first marriage and Charles would help me to raise my children.

Here I stood in my tea length wedding gown and veil, to meet this man at the minister's side whose life has also taken amazing turns. Here we are together at this very same place in our lives, ready to commit to one another. Before this time which God had appointed, there was hurt and pain, there was growth and change, and now I know that through it all, there was God.

As I began my walk to my wedding song, I used the railing for support instead of my crutch, and at the bottom of the stairs Rick waited to escort me. I was so very comfortable doing this—I knew it was time. I asked God to bless us as my mind focused on this gorgeous August day. The sky is the most beautiful blue, and the sun seemed to glow, not beam. There was a quiet breeze that very gently touched, with just a hint of coolness. I know that God had already begun to bless our marriage, beginning with this day.

As I walked down the stairs of my parents' home; chairs had been arranged in the living room with an aisle down the middle. Here our family and friends sat on either side. Charles nodded and smiled as I walked to meet him. Shelly stood as my matron of honor, and my cousin Lena as my bridesmaid. Standing with Charles was his brother Barry as his best man, and Charles, Jr., as his groomsman.

As the minister began the Lord's Prayer I thanked God for His perfect timing; my life seemed to blossom before my eyes, and then everything became so crystal clear. After the ceremony was over we went out into the yard, which was beautifully decorated with canopy covered tables and chairs.

Now our journey would begin, as I was about to get more tough lessons on the institution of marriage. We will start with the most difficult, submission. Up until now an argument wasn't over until I said it was over. I had the right to say whatever was on my mind, so of course all last words belonged to me...always. I began to study what God expects of me in my marriage, "Wives, submit yourselves unto your own husbands; as unto the Lord," (Ephesians 5:22). This would be a difficult lesson but God had already begun to work on my attitude. I have learned that if my life goal is to be obedient to God, I must be able to control my tongue and discipline my mind. This would allow me to take my rightful place beside my husband as his helper, (Genesis 2:18). I made another conscious decision to work on this, and then I committed to do it. I would have to learn to sacrifice things I may think, do or say so that I may be obedient to God. This lesson had me confront my own selfish and confrontational behavior, which did not happen overnight. This took many instances of controlling my actions and reactions to situations. I prayed for the Lord's help. Submission is discipline, and just as Jesus wasn't pleasing Himself, but God when He died on the cross, marriage is not about pleasing ourselves, but one another. Selfishness is the number one enemy of marriage. God revealed that being in submission would not make me less than my husband, and it doesn't mean that I would have to agree with everything he says. Instead I needed to learn that there is a way to handle disagreements with compromise. Marriage is a constant work and when marriages last, they last because the married couple never stopped working at it.

I used to pray for God to change my husband's attitude and to help him to be more loving. He wasn't the type to hug and snuggle. Then the most awesome truth came to me. While I was busy praying for my husband's attitude, I should have been praying for my own. Instead of asking God to help my husband to be more loving, I should have been more loving to him. I've learned that my behavior often shaped my husband's behavior, and his mine.

In marriage we are to become one, and it is possible. "Therefore shall a man leave his father and mother, and shall cleave unto his wife; and they shall be one flesh," (Genesis 2:24). Separate yet one, who better to understand the works of separate but one then our Lord, and our God? One of the most valuable lessons we've learned is not to burden each other with the responsibility for the others' happiness. Our joy comes from our own personal relationships with the Lord. As I continued to grow I began to understand God's vision for husband and wife.

Marriage is multi-dimensional and includes trials and tribulations, and it takes love, trust and commitment. I give Charles what God has given me to give him: love, trust, support, faithfulness, and respectful reminders.

God has made women wonderful and beautiful creatures, we can multitask. As wives and mothers, we work, go to school, and then we're maids, doctors, nurses, teachers, self-esteem builders and motivators and that's just in our own homes! This is a natural ability given to us by God. I know my weaknesses, and I try to allow my husband to help me. My weaknesses are his strengths, and his weaknesses are my strengths.

God made woman for man and we each have an obligation to the other, in God's eyes. "Wives, submit to your own husbands, as to the Lord," (Ephesians 5:22); "Husbands, love your wives just as Christ also loved the church and gave Himself for her,"(Ephesians 5:25). Marriage should be a reflection of the relationship between Christ and His church. These obligations are clear, and the cost of disobedience leads to divorce, adultery and fornication; these disobedient acts destroy God's perfect plan for this union. I consider our marriage a healthy, one not because it's perfect, but because it is secure in the Lord. We know now that arguments are a part of our learning experience, as long as we find a common ground. When we can not we go in different directions until we've had time to calm down and seek Lord.

It is all about acknowledging Jesus, accepting Him, seeking Him, and obeying Him. We must take seriously the comparison of marriage to the relationship between Christ and the church. Forgiveness in our relationship with Christ and forgiveness in marriage is imperative; Christ has forgiven us, and we must forgive others. Any kind of abuse would not be present in a relationship with Christ, therefore it has no place in a marriage.

As I mentioned before, marriage is constant work, and it has never proven more difficult than when our finances were in jeopardy. Charles worked for a printing company for twenty-six years when the owner decided to close the company for good. On that same day, we found out I needed to have spinal surgery. Charles had to make a decision whether to look for work now, or to wait until after my surgery because I would need a lot of care during recovery. We now had five children who depended on us. Our older children were grown and living nearby. This decision was one we could not take lightly because it would affect our standard of living. We would loose our health coverage and the bulk of our income. Charles made the decision to stay at home until I had recuperated from the surgery, and he would assume my responsibilities in our home. Charles has worked since he was old enough to scrub floors and marble steps, which he did for the elderly neighbors in our neighborhood. Now he's given up much to take care of us. Through all of my complicated health issues he washed, cooked, cleaned, and became my nurse. He learned special skills to take care of me. There were times when I could not urinate on my own and Charles had to learn how to catheterize me. He learned to lift me, to care for bedsores, bathing, medicating, and dressing me every morning and every night. Years of carrying me up and down the stairs with and without a wheelchair. Charles woke up at night to turn me from one side to the other because I didn't have the strength to do it on my own. He had to keep up with the children's doctor's appointments, school conferences and my doctor's appointments. I praise him for all he does because I realize there aren't many men who would have sacrificed all that he has for us. That's commitment! I let him know that I appreciate him.

As soon as our children could read, our morning devotions consisted of each reading two prayers out of a book of prayers for children. We constantly ask God's guidance for them, after all He is the Father of all fathers. If anyone can teach us to be the best parents that we can be, it is God. He also has an advantage over us—He created our children and knew them before they were born. They were born in the womb of God's love and we thank Him for them. I promised God that we would guide them back to Him, this is our duty as parents and that's where they belong. It is not an easy task being a parent, and if done diligently, it is the most difficult job in the world. We have learned that we must stand together as a united force, and when we don't, the children sense it and then use it to their advantage. We pray for them daily because we know the world is waiting for them when they leave the house. We constantly taught them, but we do understand that they must go through things to bring about their own life experiences. We can not shield them from life, but we do make them aware of the consequences of their decisions and actions.

We should do all we can to raise our children to know God. They will not understand now but their future will depend on their relationship with Him. "Train up a child in the way he should go, And when he is old he will not depart from it," (Proverbs 22:6).

Single parents, allow God to be the ultimate Father for your children by maintaining your own personal relationship with Jesus. This will strengthen your ability to parent with God's guidance, and will allow Him to lead you. He loves us and He knows what we need. "In all your ways acknowledge Him, and He shall direct your paths," (Proverbs. 3:6).

To Honor You

Father we need You to stand with us
As we begin our marriage on commitment
and trust. Some days will bring obstacles
we must overcome, as we learn to forgive
while bonding as one. Commitment will keep
us from going astray, and we'll remember
our love from our wedding day. We didn't
take it lightly when we vowed "I do."
Holy is this union created by You.

The Ultimate Creation

Yes, my Lord, here I stand as You've
perfected me to man. I am the woman that
You created with gifts to share to complete
my husband, for he completes me. Together
we are the ultimate creation, created in Your
image; what I am he isn't and what he is
I am not. That is Your purpose, Your divine
intention. For You, by You, with You and
in You, here we stand Man and Woman
together—we are the ultimate creation. Lord, help
my husband to understand that I can only be the
woman You've created me to be, if in Your
image he will, take care of me.

SPIRITUAL MATURITY

WHEN WE'RE SPIRITUALLY MATURE WE'RE CONFIDENT OF OUR salvation, we're resting on the promises of God, and we're experiencing a peace that can only come from Him.

There is nothing like knowing that you have the victory over a life experience. Even as you go through, you are certain of the outcome because you completely trust God. When the storm is over you can stand while blowing the dust off your feet, standing firm for the next life experience.

I became so used to going through physical trials that I began to look past the storm. The enemy took me to the threshold of death, but I wasn't afraid because I knew what was on the other side for me—*life*. Whether I woke in the spirit or in the physical body, God would make that decision. I know that I am secure.

Though I am a sinner, sin no longer has any control over my life. "For sin shall not have dominion over you, for we are not under the law but under grace." (Romans 6:14)

Spiritual maturity leads us to be Christ like "But we all, with unveiled face, beholding as in a mirror, the glory of the Lord, are being transformed into the same image from glory to glory, just as by the spirit of the Lord," (2 Corinthians 3:18). In spiritual maturity we will begin to see ourselves in the scriptures. "The Spirit Himself bears witness with our spirit that we are children of God." (Romans 6:14) This is confirmed when the spirit begins to lead and direct you. We should recognize ourselves as the Spirit transforms us to where we, as well as others, will recognize the fruit of the spirit, "But the fruit of the Spirit is love, joy, peace, longsuffering, kindness, goodness, faithfulness, gentleness, self-control. Against such there is no law," (Galatians 5:22, 23).

As we grow in spiritual maturity, we grow to be more like Christ. "As I have been crucified with Christ; it is no longer I who live, but Christ lives in me; and the life which I now live in the flesh

I live by faith in the Son of God, who loved me and gave Himself for me," (Galatians 2:20).

At some point in Jesus' younger years He became aware that He was the servant spoken of in prophecy. That He, the carpenter's son, was the Son of God and at twelve years old, Jesus knew His mission was to do His Father's business. (Luke 2:41–49). Did His earthly parents tell Him of His divine conception? Would prophecy help Him to comprehend the magnitude of His calling? Imagine this awesome revelation. His mission was revealed and then He had to comprehend it, accept it, and fulfill it. Jesus was God both in essence and in nature. He could not deviate from that, and He could not sin, because He was God. Jesus Himself proclaimed, "I and my Father are one," (John 10:30).

Life rendered Jesus the same experiences that we endure as His children. He had to overcome temptation, be rejected, talked about, be misunderstood, called a liar; He was criticized publicly and harshly, He grieved, He was scared, He cried, He struggled, felt joy, was forsaken by others; He was betrayed, imprisoned, shamed, beaten, mocked, called out of His name; Jesus was physically abused, tortured; He was hurt, saddened, humiliated, went through excruciating physical pain, and was then lifted on a cross to die. Through it all He depended on God. Jesus drew His strength from God, and we are also able to access that same exact strength through the Holy Spirit. Jesus remained faithful, devoted, loyal, steadfast, prayerful, focused, and humbled before God, and not only to God, but to you and me.

Even as He knew they were seeking to kill Him, He thought not of Himself but of others. "I do not pray for these alone, but also for those who will believe in Me through their word," (John 17:20). Jesus' focus was on a completed mission and also on His disciples who would continue His work by their testimonies of Him. "Therefore, since Christ suffered for us in the flesh, arm yourselves also with the same mind, for he who has suffered in the flesh has ceased from sin, that he no longer should live the rest of his time in the flesh for the lusts of men, but for the will of God," (1 Peter 4:1–2). Jesus completed His mission in just thirty-three years. From

Jesus' ministry came testimonies of those who witnessed His life, death, and His resurrection.

Old Testament prophecy could allow Jesus to identify Himself, just as God's blue print (the Bible) was written so that we can identify ourselves. Not only to help us to grow spiritually, but to assure us of many truths, one of which is, eternal life "These things I have written to you who believe in the name of the Son of God, that you may know that you have eternal life, and that you may continue to believe in the name of the Son of God," (1 John 5:13). Jesus' testimony was written so that we may know for sure and without doubt.

We too must accept our calling to discipline ourselves just as Jesus did. We must spend time with God and draw strength from Him. Here we can be guided into spiritual maturity and worthy of being eternally perfected in Christ. "Having therefore these promises, dearly beloved, let us cleanse ourselves from all filthiness of the flesh and spirit, perfecting holiness in the fear of God." (2 Corinthians 6:18) We should all live in fear of the wrath of God. This is the same God that sent the people he created from His presence in the garden because of disobedience (Genesis 3). We're talking about the same God that destroyed the two cities of Sodom and Gomorrah because of their sin, and who turned Lot's wife into a pillar of salt because she disobeyed by looking back, (Genesis 19:15–26). This is the God whose anger was evident against David and his affair with Bathsheba and allowed their child to die (1 Samuel 11, 12:1–18). Our sin is very serious, not only because it affects others, but because we will have to stand before God. We must understand a few things about our sin. I was taught that there are sins of omission, which we discussed earlier. They are things that we know we should do but don't do them: reading the Bible, praying, etc. Then there are sins of commission, these are things that we know are wrong but do them anyway: lying, stealing, etc.

When Adam and Eve sinned against God it separated us from Him; Jesus died to reconcile us back to God, that is true, but not so that we could continue to live in sin, on the expectation of forgiveness from God. We must allow the Holy Spirit to guide us to a relationship where we fear God because when we do not fear Him, we become comfortable with sin in ourselves and in others. "For we know Him who said, Vengeance is Mine, I will repay, says the Lord. And again, The Lord will judge His people. It is a fearful thing to fall into the hands of the living God," (Hebrews 10:30–31). Sin is to be overcome, not lived in, and Jesus made that possible. We should show our gratitude to Christ for dying on the cross by overcoming our sinfulness.

"Because it is written be holy for I am holy." (Leviticus 19:2, 1 Peter 1:16) Holiness is the state of being set apart from the world for God's use. God chose men and women and used them to make a difference in the lives of others. Moses, Noah, Deborah, Isaiah, Ezekiel, Daniel, Paul, and Timothy, they were appointed to guide His people with their visions, faithfulness, wisdom, knowledge and truth, all so we may mature spiritually. It was true then and it is true now. God has never ceased setting apart those who diligently seek Him.

Once we take our places as the children of God and begin to exercise our spiritual gifts to the glory of God, only then will we experience the true power of the church. We should all identify the gifts that God has given to us. Every person's gifts are important, and every gift should be used to serve the body of Christ. Pastors do not possess every gift, and should not be expected to hold up the church alone. This is very important if we ever expect to experience the fullness of the Lord. When our gifts are not being utilized, the body will not be properly nourished, and when the body starves it becomes weak. God can bring the same message with a different perspective through different people, and this feeds the whole body. Every gift is needed to supply a body with all it needs to survive, so that we may grow to perfection and be prepared when Jesus comes to receive us.

> "But now God has set the members, each one of them, in the body just as He pleased. And if they were all one member, where would the body be? But now indeed there are many members, yet one body. And the eye cannot say to the hand, 'I have no need of you'; nor again the head to the feet; 'I have no need of you.'" 1 Corinthians 12:18–21

Instilled

With all of Your glory You're etched In my mind;
You're the foundation of life the tie that binds.
With all of Your love You're entrenched in my heart,
Engrave Your words on my lips, whenever they part.
Empower my thoughts with Your perfect will,
In my life, in my soul Jesus, be forever instilled.

"You shall love the Lord your God with all your heart,
with all your soul, with all your strength, and with all your
mind." (Luke 10:27a)

The Cradle of God's Arms

This sweet peace I have found for it is here,
That you'll find my mind and heart. Yes it is here.
With love that soothes the trials of life, it is here.
In darkness there will be light if you will come here
Gentle days and restful nights, if you will stay here,
You will be protected if you will come here
in the cradle of God's arms.

"You will keep him in perfect peace, Whose mind is
stayed on You, Because he trusts in You." (Isaiah 26:3)

MY SHEEP HEAR MY VOICE

SINCE THE BEGINNING OF TIME GOD HAS TALKED, WALKED, instructed, rewarded and punished His people. In the garden, Adam was instructed not to eat from, "the tree of the knowledge of good and evil," (Genesis 2:17). Adam and Eve, "Heard the voice of the Lord God walking in the cool of the day,"(Genesis 3:8) They also taught their children to offer sacrifices to God, and in a fit of jealous rage Cain killed his brother which led to punishment from God. (Genesis 4:8–16) "Enoch walked with God," (Genesis 5:22, Hebrews 11:5); Noah heard God's voice and so did Samuel and other prophets. We all have the ability to hear God's voice, and if we're not, it's probably due to our busy and stressful lives. We don't give Him the time to speak to us.

In the midst of the sins of His people, God was grieved because "they thought evil continually," (Genesis 6:5). Noah found grace in the sight of God. He was a just man, and perfect in His generations. Noah was considered perfect not because he was sinless but because he loved and obeyed God with his whole heart and Noah walked with God, (Genesis 7–9). Because Noah obeyed Him, God rewarded Noah and his family. He told him to build an ark, and gave him specific measurements of the ark, told him who was to get on the ark, and to bring two of every sort of animal and creeping things, male and female. God told Noah *"to keep them alive."* He told him how long it was going to rain. Noah obeyed all he was told to do, and the "Lord shut him in," (Genesis 6, 7). After the forty days and nights of rain, the Lord set a rainbow in the sky to remember the covenant between Him and the earth, to not destroy it by water again, (Genesis 9:9–17).

God left no stone unturned and every tiny detail had to be carried out, in order for His plan to work. This was not only for Noah's family, but for mankind and every other living thing. If Noah had neglected the animals and one of them died, they would not have been able to replenish the earth. God's nature is unchanging and He can not lie, and we can rest on his promises and covenants, (Hebrews 6:18–19). God still hangs His promises for all to see just as he did the rainbow.

I remember the night before my last open heart surgery I heard Him say, "I will give you a new heart." I held on to His words because I knew His voice. I know God can not lie. Since that time, I've heard my doctors refer to my heart as "your new heart," and I have been told by several technicians doing tests on my heart that, at first glance, my heart appears to function as a normal healthy heart.

When we can hear His voice we can have much peace in His covering over us. We should anchor this truth in our souls so that we may enter the holiest of holies where all power, love and peace reign. Spending time with Him is very important to our relationship with God. I had to sacrifice some worldly things that kept me so busy that I didn't have time for God. Some of those things that I claimed to do for Him, in reality took quality time away from Him. I've learned that just as I needed time with Him everyday, He longed to spend time with me, quality time where He is the focus. Not while driving the car, or fixing dinner, those times have their place to worship Him. Time one on one is crucial to this relationship. This was the reason we were created, and even as sin separated us from God, He already had plans to reconcile us, (Ephesians 1). He has made His position very clear.

I learned to hear God's voice through my trials and tribulations, through hurt and pain, and with time spent in His presence. In diligently seeking God, I found Him. "But from there you will seek the Lord your God, and you will find Him if you seek Him with all your heart and with all your soul," (Deuteronomy 4:29).

I prayed for discernment, that I may know His voice from other voices that sometimes deceived me. While spending time in His presence He cleaned, polished and refined my gift to hear Him and the more I obeyed, the more He strengthened my desire to obey. I've learned that God rewards us for being obedient, just as He rewarded Daniel for His obedience, (Daniel 1). When the Spirit lives in us, we can communicate and know and even speak the mind of Christ. "But he who is spiritual judges all things, yet he himself is rightly judged by no one. For who has known the mind of the Lord that he may instruct Him? But we have the mind of Christ," (1 Corinthians 2:15–16).

In all that I have gone through God was molding me to do a work that is finally becoming clear to me. He used my pain and illnesses to teach me to pay great attention to tiny details. This has carried over into my everyday life, and is proving very important for what God has planned for my life. I must hear, and to act accordingly to the way He has instructed. I've learned that hearing means to process, to understand, to comprehend; hearing is action. "If anyone has an ear let him hear," (Revelations 13:9). God delivered me from a state of selective hearing, where I heard what I wanted to hear. Now I hear His voice through the Holy Spirit.

The first time He instructed me to do something I had more excuses than Moses. "Who am I that I should speak for You? What if no one believes me?" I'm not used to talking to people! I can't walk good enough to do this! Just as God told Moses, if they don't believe you then say this, or do that. Just like Moses, I had to do what I was told, (Exodus 4). God said that He would be with me and I learned very quickly that if I don't do it, I don't sleep. I don't rest because I have not obeyed. After I have obeyed, God reveals scripture where He used people to do, or to say the same thing. Sometimes I will cross paths with others who have had the same assignment within the body of Christ. It was then that I realized another truth from the word of God: "Jesus Christ is the same yesterday, today, and forever," (Hebrews 13:8). I believe that if you want to know what's going to happen in our future, look in the Old Testament. He will always remain the same.

I took notice that my prayer life was stronger after the Comfort Zone. I've learned that while praying in the Spirit, it will only ask those things which are in God's will. This is because it is the mind of Christ. Praying isn't just for our personal relationship, but also to serve others in intercessory prayer. I learned that my spiritual health determines how I handle all things—physically, mentally and emotionally. Our spiritual health and discipline is needed to control our human desires.

Some doubt that we can hear Him, but Jesus makes it clear that He does speak with us. He speaks to us through His word, sermons, hymns and through others. Once we know His voice we can not be fooled by any other voice; we may hear them but we will not follow them. "My sheep hear My voice, and I know them, and they follow Me. And I give them eternal life, and they shall never parish; neither shall anyone snatch them out of my hand. My Father, who has given them to Me, is greater than all; and no one is able to snatch them out of My Father's hand,"(John 10:27–29).

No other voice could have gotten me out of my bed of affliction or place new life into my legs. Only the voice of God could have promised me a new heart. No other voice could have given me words of wisdom and insight to serve others in His name, and with His guidance. No other voice can guide us to the truths of who we truly are in Christ because no other voice wants us to know. Though I have suffered, studied and endured for years, praying for God to mold me, and to use me to His glory. I realized that though I work hard to shed my old self for my new self, that just like Jesus I am still subject to criticism by someone else's carnal thinking and carnal wisdom. That's why we must be sure of whose we are and to whom we belong. Others may not know what we've gone through to be able to serve God. Many didn't believe Jesus, but I've learned from my own life that God can use any one at any time for any purpose He chooses. He is God!

Eli was already a priest when God called Samuel as a boy and gave Samuel a vision about the fate of Eli and his sons because of their behaviors, which Eli didn't correct. Although Samuel was just a boy, Eli who was a priest and judge recognized that Samuel could hear God. He wanted to hear what God spoke to Samuel about him. Eli was preoccupied with the created presence of God (the Ark of the Covenant) more than with His real and spiritual presence. This happens to many of us, we get caught up in the rituals, and the how we've always done it. We don't even realize that the real presence of the spiritual God has left us. Just like the Pharisees in Jesus' time, they held on so tightly to Moses' law, that they didn't recognize the prophet that Moses prophesied would come—Jesus, (Genesis 22:18, Deuteronomy 18:15–19). They claimed to know Moses' law and lived by all that Moses taught, yet they did not recognize the seed of Abraham who through all the nations of the earth would be blessed, (Genesis 22:18).

When we truly hear our God speak we will hear the commandments, "You shall love the Lord your God with all your heart, with all your soul, and with all your mind, This is the first and great commandment. And the second is like it; you shall love your neighbor as yourself," On these two commandments hang all the Law and the Prophets," (Matthew 22:37–40). If we love the Lord as the first commandment asks us to, and love our neighbors as the second asks. We will have obeyed all Ten Commandments.

We have all been hurt in this life; we have been wrongfully accused, raped, molested, beaten, cast aside, cheated on, and the hurts go on and on. If we could hear God we would hear the call to forgive. "But if you do not forgive men their trespasses, neither will your Father forgive your trespasses," (Matthew 6:15). Forgiveness is very important in our relationship with Jesus. When we are unable to forgive it turns into anger aimed at ourselves. It dictates how we live our lives, and eats at the core of who we are. We find that we can't love, and we become depressed, and that makes it very hard to handle everyday life. We must learn that we seldom hurt the people who have wronged us by not forgiving them. If we could hear God we could learn to live again, learn to love and trust again.

When we hear God's voice He may give us directions to lead armies to war just as He did with David, or He may send us on a mission to foreign lands. He may send us to deliver a hug or a word of comfort. Whatever the call, let us be ready to hear and to obey. "Yet they will by no means follow a stranger, but will flee from him, for they do not know the voice of strangers," (John 10:5).

Yes, I Hear You

Yes, I hear You my God, I will do all that You ask of me. I have heard Your word, which has promised to set me free. Yes, I hear You, and I will obey all that You command, Even though I can't comprehend and I may not understand. I will still obey and I will lay my understanding before You. Yes I hear You Lord for in You I will rest all of my cares. I hear You and You won't give me more than I can bear. Yes I will love my neighbors as You have asked in Your word. Yes I hear You and my life will reflect all that I have heard. All to show that I do hear You.

Love One Another

> Love one another as God loves you,
> This is what He's asked us to do.
> To spread that love far and wide,
> Allowing Him to be your guide.
> And as you spread His love around,
> What blessed joy you will have found.

WITNESS

We are all witnesses to God's grace and mercy whether we realize it or not. Saul was and continues to be a witness. His journey began to persecute all those who believed in the Lord, but Saul became a believer when he met the Lord while traveling on the road to Damascus, after which a now submissive Saul was told where to go. Because his sight had been taken away at the conclusion of the meeting the men who were to help Saul bring Christians to persecution (who were also witnesses because they heard the voice of the Lord but seeing no one), led him to where the Lord said that he should go. Meanwhile the Lord also spoke to Ananias and told him to go to a street called Straight at the house of Judas for one called Saul who came from Tarsus, and the Lord told Ananias that Saul was praying. The Lord had already given Saul a vision of a man named Ananias coming to lay hands on him and immediately Saul received his sight as scales fell from his eyes and he was filled with the Holy Spirit.

Now Ananias heard about Saul and his behavior to persecute anyone who believed in the Lord and he brought that to Jesus' attention; "Jesus said for him to go, for the Lord had chosen Saul as His vessel," (Acts 9). Ananias was obedient to the Lord although he didn't understand. Both of these men were prepared by God. Ananias had to deny what he felt and thought about Saul to do the will of the Lord, and Saul had to accept what Jesus called him to do (the total opposite of what he had been doing). Ananias had served the Lord for some time and Saul had just heard from the Lord for the first time three days prior. He gave them both visions and revelations to bring about His plan for their lives. God changed Saul's name to Paul and he became a mighty witness to all of God's wisdom, knowledge and understanding.

This is God's perfect design to use His children for the good of the church, which is not a building but a body of believers. "For as the body is one and has many members, but all the members of that one body, being many, are one body, so also is Christ," (1 Corinthians 12:12). I'm also a witness to a faithful God who promised us a comforter, a helper to assist us in becoming more like Christ with power through the Holy Spirit, (John 16:7–8, Acts 1:8).

"And we are His witnesses to these things, and so also is the Holy Spirit whom God has given to those who obey Him," (Acts 5:32). "The Holy Spirit is indeed the spirit of truth who is a teacher who will teach us about Jesus," (John 15:26). Jesus' testimony helps us to know who we are and can be and our testimonies can help others to find out who they are.

I am a witness that He will be our strength when we are weak (2 Corinthians 12:9), and that if you endure and do not get tired of going through, but go through with faith and patience, you will inherit the promises of God, (Hebrews 6:11–12).

We are all witnesses—God has delivered us and our families and friends from cancer, drugs, prison, physical and sexual abuse, domestic violence, paralysis and all manner of mental bondage, physical sickness and broken marriages. "Yet in all these things we are more than conquerors through Him who loved us," (Romans 8:37). We are conquerors and we have the ability to overcome anything through Christ.

Life experiences are meant to bring us into closer fellowship with God, and to become testimonies to others of God's love, grace and mercy. Yet these same things can be used to divert our attention from God, so that we may waddle in self-pity and depression. We must try not to fall into such traps and if we do Jesus says; "Behold, I give you authority to trample on serpents and scorpions, and over all the power of the enemy, and nothing shall by any means hurt you." (Luke 10:19). The enemy will try to use these things against us. "But as for you, you meant evil against me; but God meant it for good…" (Genesis 50:20). The enemy has no power over us if we are in Christ, and we must learn to use the power that He gives us through the Holy Spirit.

I am a witness to the fulfilled promise of the Holy Spirit, who will assist us in changing our lives and helps us to continue to live in that power. Paul made it clear that he would not be impressed with words, but with the power. "But I will come to you shortly, if the Lord wills, and I will know not the word of those who are puffed up, but the power. For the kingdom of God is not in word but in power," (1 Corinthians 4: 19–20). When the power is working it is effective and brings results. Paul tells us, "…of which I became a minister according to the gift of the grace of God given to me by the effective working of His power," (Ephesians 3:7).

In order for us to know where we're going we need to acknowledge where God has brought us from. We have battle scars that remind us of all the Lord has seen us through and we have been witnesses to miracles right up there with "rise and walk, and Lazarus come forth." How can we witness these miracles and not have them make a change in our lives? We have brain surgeries being performed, with some patients coming out of twenty years of comatose state, with no long term complications. We are witnesses and we must be alert and acknowledge God's hand in our lives. If you believe that you're not a witness, look around you; look at our perfectly engineered bodies that work in sync to keep us inhaling and exhaling the oxygen that He placed in the air for our second by second survival. There are billions of cells within our bodies, each having its own duty to keep us healthy, and even to renew parts of our bodies every second. Try to comprehend the awesome love of a Father who would give His only Son to die for foolish, disobedient and selfish children who barely speak to Him, spend time with Him, and most times won't acknowledge that He even exists. That is the love of God!

We are witnesses every day to His grace and mercy and we need to share with one another what God has done for us. This is testimony time! We need to dedicate time in our relationship with Jesus to enhance our spiritual gifts to bring support to the kingdom; and to use this fruit of the spirit, which is Christ like character. "But the fruit of the Spirit is love, joy, peace, longsuffering, kindness, goodness, faithfulness, gentleness, self-control. Against such there is no law," (Galatians 5:22). These are truly our strongest witness to Christ—our changing lives and the usage of our spiritual gifts. I'm a witness that His gifts and His power begin in His perfected love, which never fails, (1 Corinthians. 13).

I'm a witness that "I can do all things through Christ who strengthens me..." (Philippians 4:13). I am a witness that when you become an obedient child of God His promises are released in your life and going through life experiences produce patience, character and hope, just as Romans 5:3–4 says it will. We must become witnesses before we can witness. Witnessing to others has to be done in the state of being a witness. We can not win souls for Christ if we are unsure of our own salvation. I'm a witness believing that if you truly seek God you will find Him; if you develop a personal relationship with Jesus the Holy Spirit will guide you to the truth. Then Jesus said to those Jews who believed Him, "If you abide in My word, you are My disciples indeed. And you shall know the truth, and the truth shall make you free," (John 8:31–32).

I am a witness that material things mean absolutely nothing and are most times used by the enemy to control us. The more we want the more we work, the more we work the less time we have with God, Jesus warns us,

> Do not lay up for yourselves treasures on earth, where moth and rust destroy and where thieves break in and steal; but lay up for yourselves treasures in heaven, where neither moth nor rust destroys and where thieves do not break in and steal. For where your treasure is, there your heart will be also." (Matthew 6:20–21)

I am a witness that stand-up hugs meant more to my children than anything material, and that matters of the heart do more to fill the space in our souls than anything material. I am a witness that all that I have gone through I will go through again for a chance to serve God in spirit and in truth and to acknowledge Him as Lord of my life. I am proud to be running the race of life because I too have become a witness to His power and Glory. "Therefore we also, since we are surrounded by so great a cloud of witnesses, Let us lay aside every weight, and the sin which so easily ensnares us, and let us run with endurance the race that is set before us," (Hebrews 12:1).

I'm a Witness

I'm a witness for You, Lord,
I'm going to lift Your name.
I will share the victory,
That I am not the same.
I'll tell the world of Your love,
And Your earthly trials,
And how You walked to spread
God's word for so many miles.
I'm a witness to Your mercy,
I need it every day.
I want to live my life for You
Do with me what You may.

Inspired

I'm inspired by Your grandeur, the world is in Your hands,
Your every thought is action and instantly a plan. You breathed
the breath of life in us, our spirits were filled, and everything that
exists does so all because You willed. I'm inspired by your love so
unwavering and true. And all of life's miracles are all because of You.
I'm inspired by Your creations of the spirit and of flesh, with just a
word from You eternal life we will cherish. You sacrificed Your Son,
for sins He had not done, then You raised Him up again to be our
spiritual companion.

REVEALED

Some years ago I was invited to speak at the young people's prayer breakfast, and I spoke of my younger days before my paralysis.

"I loved to dance and my love for dancing encouraged my club presence which became a part of my social life. The legal age to go to the club then was eighteen. At age twenty-one I became paralyzed from the waist down due to spinal surgery. It was from my wheelchair that I learned to walk with God.

"Due to a second spinal surgery, I was sent for rehabilitation and because of an accident during a procedure in that hospital, I was in a coma for seven weeks. There was talk of disconnecting the ventilator, but before that happened I regained consciousness.

"If I can leave anything with you, I would ask you to obey your parents and your elders. We want the very best for you. Please know that whatever you're going through we have already gone through. Know that God, who is the author of our lives, is always with you. He was with me as I stood at the banks of death. When my heart and my lungs failed me, God was there. As I finished I stretched my arms to either side and said, 'Behold the Glory of the Lord!' I heard clapping as I rolled away in my wheelchair."

How could I sit there and claim to be the glory of the Lord? That five minute speech began a journey to discover why I would puff myself up like that, and using that phrase "Behold the glory of the Lord," this was so out of character for me, it just seemed to slip out. I kept thinking *That's exactly why Satan got kicked out of heaven.* I thought to myself. I asked God to forgive me for my time of weakness in thinking too much of myself. He began to lead me through the Bible to some truths about His children. I discovered that I had to go back to seeing myself as God sees me. I had to remind myself of what David also knew. "God knows all about me, He formed me and I am fearfully and wonderfully made. He saw my substance before I was even formed. His works are marvelous and He made the days for me, not me for the days. My soul does well know His love for me," (Psalm 139:13–16).

When sin cut me off from my Father (Genesis 3), God sacrificed His only Son (John 3:16). Jesus promised that after He ascended to His Father, that He would send the Holy Spirit. "But when the Helper comes, whom I shall send to you from the Father, the Spirit of truth who proceeds from the Father, He will testify of Me," (John 15:26). He also promised that if we believe (trust) in Him we will have everlasting life, (John 6:47). From God's magnificent love, through Jesus, we arc His children. Others may not recognize us because they didn't know Him (Jesus) (1 John 3:1). Even the Priests and those who studied the teachings of Moses were convinced that Jesus was just a deranged man. Here Jesus stood before them, and they did not know Him. They assumed to know where He was from and other information about Him, which teaches us that everything isn't as it may appear. As we grow closer to God we become more like Jesus; when we become His children we are joint heirs with Christ, (Romans 8:17). "We are a royal priesthood, a holy nation, His own special people," (1 Peter 2:9). I do not have to look at my righteousness as filthy rags as Isaiah did. (Isaiah 64:6). "For He made Him who knew no sin to be sin for us, that we might become the righteousness of God in Him (Jesus)," (1 Corinthians 5:21).

"Therefore I have reason to glory in Christ Jesus in the things which pertains to God," (Romans 15:17). It was not selfishness on my part when I proclaimed to be the glory of the Lord, it was the Holy Spirit inside of me, and I know now that my life is, the glory of the Lord. In raising Lazarus from his death, God's glory was exhibited, (John 11:40). His glory was also poured out in the healing of the blind man, (John 9:24). Whenever God reveals himself as all that He is and does in us, this is a manifestation of His glory. This revelation helped me to understand all He's done, and continues to do, physically, mentally, spiritually, and that others see in or through us is "the glory of the Lord." I asked God to help me to accept my identity in Him with humbleness.

Now I wanted to step into who my Father says that I am. Yes, I am a sinner, but by the blood of Christ I am redeemed. I will not see myself through the eyes of the world, but through the eyes of my Father. I understand that we are priceless to our Father, each and every one of us. Once again He would give proof of His Word, through scripture which says, "All things work together for the good of those who love God, to those who are called according to His purpose," (Romans 8:28).

As I look back over my life I can see a deliberate road map, which led me to where I am right now. Although this is a map for my life, we each have one. There are places in my life that I will call defining moments that led me to a deeper trust in God. These defining moments are recognized now as the footprints of my Father God, and His perfect will for my life. As I look back, I see these footprints from the day that I was born. It was known then that I had a hole in my heart, but surgery was put off until I was seven years old. I believe God sent angels to my dreams to comfort me. He thought it not robbery to use a little girl's worldly belief in Santa to rouse me to consciousness after that surgery, with anticipation of Christmas. The Lord introduced me to my husband when I was seven years old. He was my friend whose well wishes were amongst the ones that my Mom brought to the hospital. His brother, Frankie, had the same heart surgery a few years before. After his surgery they found that he needed another heart surgery, but he died before they could do it. This was the first common bond that I can remember between us. My husband needed to know me very well; he needed to experience my illnesses from the beginning.

What a foundation God laid for my life, all the way to my husband. He sent me back to school to my second grade class after my first open heart surgery to a caring and loving second grade teacher, who by example planted seeds of compassion in my heart; her love and caring stayed with me. I searched for her years later, and today she still shares and encourages me. I was a mother at a young age, and though I am truly blessed, this is my testimony for other young ladies. Guard your decisions, and know that choices that you make when you are a teenager do not go away when you are forty-something. Your decisions travel your life with you, and could well affect generations after you.

As God continues to reveal His awesome hand in my life, He

showed me a time when I was discouraged because I wanted a big family. I doubted, and I cried because I believed that it would not happen because of my medical problems. "Trust in the Lord with all your heart and lean not on your own understanding;" (Proverbs 3:5a). I had not a clue what God had already planned for my life. I became a foster/adoptive parent and He chose my children. There were some that I thought would stay but didn't. I'm sure He took my limitations into careful consideration. When I was told that I had three hours to live, I responded, "God has sent children to me who have already been through enough. He will not take me from them." God used my little boys as my hope to live, along with my faith in Him. I knew that He sent those children to us to make their lives better, not to destroy or confuse them. I was persistent because I knew my Lord, and no threat of my dying could change what I knew in my heart. Revealed is God's power—in all of His wonderful and marvelous ways, He began to prepare me when I was very young.

I began to talk to my doctors about my life; I noticed that I had ordered hospital records, kept diaries and notes almost from the beginning. For His plan I fell in love with words. I could not have known that they would be used to pen this memoir. Or that the poems that were written twenty-five years before would totally blend into the subject of my book today. Now I understand that though I did not know, our all knowing God did know. His footprints are plain.

Revealed is the decision of a medical team, with a patient who was teetering between life and death. I had not responded to any other antibiotic, and the only one left for consideration, was Vancomycin. Previously I had an allergic reaction to it during my heart valve infection (p.15). I can only imagine this decision making process, should they try it or not? After speaking with my family who gave them permission, the doctors gave me the medication. They expected it to further complicate my near death state. This time it had no authority over my body, there was no allergic reaction. Instead it was one of the turning points in my recovery, another footprint.

Revelations continued with the confirmations amidst the smiles and head nods when I spoke of the Comfort Zone. There were signs of disbelief, and some passed my experience off as a dream. But there were things that can not be explained. For example, as I regained consciousness there was heaviness, even a sorrow. I felt this way when leaving the sinless, to enter into the sinful. Then there was a feeling that I was glowing, which went on for more than two weeks. It diminished with time, but never completely left me. I remember speaking to a man of God about this glow.

"I really can't explain it," I said. I looked for the same expression on his face that I had become accustomed to when speaking of the Comfort Zone.

"Like Moses?" he asked.

"Who?" I asked.

"When Moses came down from Mt. Sinai the people couldn't look at him because there was a glow about him. Moses placed a veil over his face when he was before the people," (Exodus 34:29–35). Immediately I remembered the movie *The Ten Commandments* and the look on Moses' face when he came down from the mountain. That stare was the way that I felt, coming from the realm of the Comfort Zone. Weakness, frailty and sickness were my veil. Why had I not thought of Moses before? Moses came down from the presence of God, with God's glory still on him. If He would cover Moses with His glory for receiving the law, how much more will He show His glory on each of His children, who would trust and believe in His Son's life, death and resurrection?

God's glory can illuminate us until the day that we are living in His continuous light of eternal life. I prayed and thanked God as I continued to seek Him. I prayed for Him to help me to find someone from His word who was in His presence. My prayers were answered almost immediately, as Enoch was placed on my heart, and I began to search scriptures. There was nothing extraordinary about Enoch other than the fact that he walked with God, (Genesis 5:21–24).

"Now by faith Enoch was translated that he should not see death; and was not found, because God had translated him: for before his translation he had this testimony, that he pleased God," (Hebrews 11:5). I read on: "But without faith it is impossible to please Him: for he that cometh to God must believe that he is, and that he is a rewarder of them that diligently seek Him," (Hebrews 11:6). Faith in God was the source of my strength just as with Enoch. I wanted to know more about him when someone mentioned a book in which Enoch's testimony of being taken up not once, but twice. I understand that God's desire and purpose in my life is for me to become more Christ like. He wants me to actually be in nature the image of our Savior and Lord. So just as he rewarded Enoch for walking with Him, then surely shielding me from death in the Comfort Zone was a reward for being obedient. I maintained a personal relationship with Him, despite my trials and tribulations.

Revealed is the life of Job, this is a testimony of a faithful servant. The enemy went before God and in a conversation about Job, God praises him for being a faithful servant. The enemy however assures God that the only reason Job is faithful is because God has blessed him with wealth. So God allowed the enemy to cause Job to loose his wealth in one day. He lost his family, home, land, servants and livestock. Job grieved but was still faithful to God, and understood that those things could be replaced. "Naked I came from my mother's womb, and naked I shall return there. The Lord gave, and the Lord has taken away; blessed be the name of the Lord," (Job 1:21). Again the enemy went before God. He spoke of Job's faithfulness, and the enemy said: Yes, he passed with the material things, but if you allow his health to fail, You will see…and he will surely curse you to your face!"(Job 2:5b). God gave the enemy permission to touch his health, but He told him: "Behold, he is in your hand, but spare his life," (Job 2:6). Job was struck with boils from head to toe, and his wife told him to curse God and die. Job's friends tried to get him to confess his sins, because they thought that all of his troubles were punishment, (Job 2). Job's friends were busy analyzing, and complicated the situation by trying to understand the reason for Job's current issues. Job cursed the day that he was born, but he did not curse God. Job's friends should have been supportive; they were willing to stay with Job and to pray with him, but not once did they truly place the situation in God's hands, as they kept trying to figure it all out. This made God angry with Job's three friends, because they judged Job when he had not sinned. Job went through it all while showing unwavering faith in the Lord. Then Job went to God on the behalf of his friends so that God would forgive them. Because of Job's faith, God restored his wealth to more than He had before. God also gave him a beautiful family, (Job 42).Yes, God will reward us.

As the president of the New Member's Ministry at my church home, we were often rewarded for our faithful service with very special people whom God sent to us. There's one new member who was sent and continues to encourage me with words of confirmation from the Lord. She joined our church almost a year after Ma-Ma died. Mrs. Bailey has sustained a personal relationship with the Lord from a very young age. We both felt a spiritual connection. In talking she used some of the same words Ma-Ma used to when talking to me. In sharing our testimonies, I revealed a small portion of my experience in the Comfort Zone. Without even thinking she said: "Just think of how you must have pleased God for Him to allow you even a glimpse, of what He has for us, it's awesome to even think about," the exact words *"pleased God,"* referring to Enoch in Hebrews 11:5. God confirms everything.

God has gifted me with wisdom and knowledge and a heart that openly sought out the same. I could not get enough of His word, and I asked God for more confirmations. Over the course of a few years, God revealed remnants of the teachings from the Comfort Zone, which are directly linked to scripture. While they are numerous, I chose to use "water" to share with you here. I had depended on other drinks, tea, soda, lemonade to supply my body with water. I was never in the habit of drinking clear water. This all changed when I was taught in the Comfort Zone that God uses water both in symbol and in natural order. We use water as a symbol to cleanse us of our sins (baptism) on the outside. Drinking pure water is also a God given cleanser, and helps to wash away harmful germs and toxins from the inside of our bodies. Jesus used it in His first miracle by turning it into good wine, (John 2:7–10). He spoke of water as a symbol of spiritual fulfillment and eternal life, (John 4:14). Jesus took the place of the water in the pool in the healing of the lame man, (John 5:3–9). He referred to "Living Water," as in the "Holy Spirit," (John 7:37–39). He made an example of how we are to serve one another, and to remember our places in serving Him by washing His disciples' feet with water, (John 13:5–15). As the soldiers pierced Jesus' side with a spear, there was water, symbolizing baptism, being the beginning of His ministry; and blood, symbolizing the end of His ministry. It is all perfectly planned by He who is the beginning and the end; The Alpha and Omega who is the First and the Last.

The Holy Spirit led me to still more scripture, confirming the knowledge I gained in the Comfort Zone. Years later as I explained to someone about how clear and beautiful the water was in the Comfort Zone, and the spirit led me to this scripture: "And He showed me a pure river of water of life, clear as crystal, proceeding from the throne of God and the Lamb of God," (Revelations 22:1).

I learned in the Comfort Zone that we complicate everything by leaning on our own understanding. I've learned to take God's word for what it means—nothing more and nothing less. While studying I ask Him to shed light on the scriptures, and to guide me to His truth.

Revealed are the New Testament writers who bring us the testimony of Jesus, and of their own personal relationship with Him. I am intrigued by their wisdom in love, in Christian character, in faithfulness, and in their passion to carry out the will of God in their lives. None of these men could have written what was on God's heart if God was not in control of their lives. God spoke to them and He reveals to us. We must be prepared with a personal relationship with Him, so that we can understand and accept these revelations. The Bible says: "All scripture is given by inspiration of God, and is profitable for doctrine, for reproof, for correction, for instruction in righteousness, that the man of God may be complete, thoroughly equipped for every good work,"(2 Timothy 3:16–17). He has given us all we need to be complete, to be righteous and to be equipped. His spirit dwells inside of us. He has also given His word which was inspired by Him, through His people.

God is waiting to shower us with gifts, love, and rewards beyond our carnal comprehension. We can not with our carnal love, carnal thinking, and carnal ways have a relationship with a spiritual God. I've learned that we can not limit our belief in God to how we think. We will not find Him boxed up in our worldly thinking, or in our own agendas. In the supernatural realm is where we'll find the unsurpassed knowledge of God. Here we will have to throw away what we see for what we feel and hear.

"For to be carnally minded is death, but to be spiritually minded is life and peace. Because the carnal mind is enmity against God; for it is not subject to the law of God, nor indeed can be,"(Romans 8:6–7). Having to see evidence of everything is destroying the foundation to our relationship with God. He uses His power in ways that we cannot see or even understand. "For we walk by faith, not by sight," (2 Corinthians 5:7). How many times have you been in a situation that seemed hopeless? Then you were relieved to find that Jesus has worked it out, in His way, and in His time. You could not see Him working it out, but He did. This is where I learned that everything is not what it seems.

I know that Pharaoh didn't know who he was dealing with in not letting the children of Israel go. He had to be shown God's power in the Plaques of locusts, hail, cattle dying, water turning to blood. I'm sure the children of Israel felt that there was no way out, and thought they were trapped at the Red Sea, (Exodus 7, 8, 9, 10). It is out of our realm of thinking to believe that the sea will part, to expose dry land to allow you to cross the span of the sea. I know that King Nebuchadnezzar had no idea when he sent Shadrach, Meshach, and Abednego to a fiery furnace that was seven times hotter at his request, and they walked out of the fiery furnace unburned, that the king would be converted to worship their God, (Daniel 3).

Things are not always what they seem and I remember an experience that made me feel that way. When my son, Allen, was seventeen months old I remember getting out of the car on a very windy day. I walked with my crutches. Every time I lifted my crutches to take a step, the wind would grab my crutch, and little Allen's body. I remember praying, *God please help us to the door,* which was still quite a distance away. A strange man walked up to me whose clothes were tattered, torn and dirty. His beard and moustache seemed to be matted, and he wore a dirty cap on his head. I was afraid to talk to him because of how he appeared. "You need help to the building with your boy?" he asked. He must have sensed my apprehension. "Don't worry, it is okay," he said.

My mind began to race as I imagined he would take my child and run. Then I noticed that in his helping me, he seemed to know exactly what assistance I needed. He had me transfer both crutches to one arm, and he picked Allen up and held my hand. As soon as he had everything under control he began to praise God. "God takes care of His own," the man said.

"Yes He certainly does, He is an Awesome God!" I replied. Our conversation went on until we reached the door. I was really comfortable with this stranger as he put Allen down on the floor. "Thank you so very much," I said.

With his finger towards the sky, "All honor to God, all honor to God," he said, walking away. The scripture came to mind: "Do not forget to entertain strangers, for by so doing some have unwittingly entertained angels," (Hebrews 13:2).

I did not think for one minute that this man could have been an angel. In my own carnal thinking, I could not have considered that God saw me struggling and sent help to me. I judged this man because of his outward appearance, and we judge one another according to our carnal beliefs. Revealed was the heart of the man, his reverence of God and that he well could have been an angel. Revealed is the mind altering process from carnal thinking to spiritual thinking. This prepared me to accept my supernatural relationship with Christ.

I am Here

I am here through all of your storms,
Through the trials of life, to the deepest depths.

I am here, search no more for someone to love you, to comfort you,; I know you better than you know yourself, I know what you need in blessings and wealth. I am here, I will never break your heart, Yes I said never. My love will not fade, because it endures forever. I am Jesus, I am here.

I am His Child

I am a child of God, I am a queen, a princess, a star, a servant, a peasant; I am an heir to God's throne, and this is who I am! I have been given power to help change lives, lift spirits, change hearts, bring a word, heal a soul, and to move mountains. This is who I am! I will praise Him for He is awesome, I will follow Him wherever He leads, He made me all that I am, with all of His power He has; I am His child. God is Almighty, I will honor His presence, and I will bow down, He will always be my Master, my Comforter, my Lord, my Father, and I…am His child.

FAITH/ THE KEY

Many of us struggle with faith because of our human desire to need proof of everything; we are unable to move inside of the kind of faith that we need to trust in God. "Faith is the substance of things hoped for, the evidence of things not seen," (Hebrews 11:1). Learning to depend on God comes with storms and inside of these storms is where I earned patience as I prayed for peace and faith to endure. I had to remember that no matter how bad the storm appeared to be, even when death is lurking, God can protect you in a place where death can not go.

"So faith comes by hearing and hearing by the word of God," (Romans 10:17). Through reading, music, sermons, and study, I began to hear the word of God, and through hearing I learned to live the word, which developed my faith in Him. This took deliberate action from me to learn and to apply the word to my life, and to allow the Holy Spirit to change me because I wanted to please God. Faith has opened my eyes to His magnificent truths. As the shepherd of his father's sheep, David often summoned God for protection against lions and bears who attempted to eat the sheep. This left David with a memorable history of God's faithfulness in protecting him. This history of God's faithfulness gave David courage to face what an entire army of men was afraid to do—to go one on one with the Philistine Goliath. David knew that he would be victorious although he was a boy and Goliath was a man and almost ten feet tall, (1 Samuel 17:26–51).

David said, "You come to me with a sword, with a spear, and with a javelin. But I come to you in the name of the Lord of hosts, the God of the armies of Israel, whom you have defied," (1 Samuel 17:45). David depended on God for protection and had grown very used to it. He had grown fearless in the face of anything against him. David did not have to wonder if God would protect him, he knew that He would because He is a faithful God. David was at a serious disadvantage, but He slew the giant with one single shot from a sling shot. David knew His God would be there. When we follow David's example by facing the lions, and bears of life, by standing fearless before every storm, we too will become fearless.

There are times when we know that a storm is approaching, and others may pop up with no warning. That was what happened to me when I was informed that I had only hours to live. No matter how they may come we must be armed with God as our protector. "As for God, His way is perfect; the word of the Lord is proven; He is a shield to all who trust in him," (Psalm 18:30). When we are properly armed we can do battle at any moment, and it doesn't mean that we won't ever be afraid, or that we won't ever cry or be tired. However, it does mean that even while we are afraid, we continue to believe and trust in God, and know that He is with us even when it feels as though He is not. "I will not leave you nor forsake you," (Hebrews 13:5). It's during those times that I had to remember to hold on tighter to His words. I had to pray more, read more, sing more and praise Him more. We should remember to use our prior knowledge of our faithful God to build upon our faith. If God kept me through the last storm then He will keep me through the next, I remembered, and that kept me through my trials and tribulations. God is a faithful God.

When King Darius was considering placing Daniel in charge of the whole realm, the governors and others who didn't want Daniel to be elevated to that position conspired against him. They constructed a royal statute, a firm decree that couldn't be changed even by the king himself, that if anyone was caught praying to any god or man except for King Darius for thirty days, they would be cast into the lions den. They knew that Daniel prayed three times a day every day. Again the governor and others conspired to catch Daniel while praying to God, and they did. Although the king respected Daniel's relationship with his God, he could not keep him from the lions den. King Darius said before the stone was rolled in front of the door. "Your God, whom you serve continually, He will deliver you." And he did, God sent angels to shut the mouths of the lions, (Daniel 6:1–23). The king was very pleased when Daniel was still alive the next morning. Daniel must have represented his God very well even the king believed that Daniel's God would deliver him from the lions, and when He did king Darius made a decree that his kingdom will tremble and fear the God of Daniel, (Daniel 6:23–28). Daniel's faith had infected others around him. I wanted the faith of David when he went one on one with the giant; I wanted his courage when he continued to honor God even though he knew that he would be sent to the lions den, (Daniel 6:6–28).

Are we representing God so well that others wish to know Him? Are we sharing our faith to encourage others? Are we a good representation of the one true God who can speak to the water and it will gather to make oceans, seas, lakes and rivers? Who can collect dry land to make continents and countries? A God who can speak to a storm and it will cease, the only one who can dissolve the darkness in the universe or inside of us, and bring it to the marvelous light. Are we setting an example of faith for others to imitate? (Hebrews 6:12). Paul saw this infectious faith in Timothy when he said: "When I call to remembrance the genuine faith that is in you, which dwelt first in your grandmother Lois and your mother Eunice, and I am persuaded is in you also," (2 Timothy 1:5).

Without my knowledge my great-grandmother and grandmother's faith was the example in which my faith began to grow. They prayed in our presence and without our knowledge their example became our foundation. These two women were faith in action, living faith, infectious faith, they didn't possess many material things but they had what mattered—faith in an awesome God. There are testimonies of the faithful in God's word, (Hebrews 11). These are ordinary people who affirmed their faith in God, in extraordinary ways, and God continues to make promises to His people. I remember the night before my last open heart surgery, when I heard Him say, "I will give you a new heart," and "This is your last major obstacle." When I heard those words I didn't have to think twice. I repeated those words to everyone who would listen without hesitation. When God spoke those words, peace filled my soul, my eyes filled with tears and my spirit quickened to fulfillment. It has been six years since His promise to me, and they have been the healthiest years of my entire life. No major obstacles, and that is what He promised. That's why I pray to live every day of my life to reflect Him, in displaying His character, His love, His faith-fulness—it's all to His glory. He is still a covenant making God. As I mentioned before, some medical personnel refer to my heart as my "new heart," not because they know of the night God spoke to me, but because God confirms through others what He has said in His own exact words. No one could have assured me of my health but God. No one could have gotten me from my bed after years of paralysis but God, and surely no one could have shielded me from death, but God. He etched His words on my heart and I pray to be all He has created me to be.

In this evidence awareness world, faith calls us to believe in what we can not see. This supernatural relationship with God focuses on a reliance upon God's word. "For without faith it is impossible to please God," (Hebrews 11:6). Faith is a hope with an expectation of delivery in God's time. It asks us to be available to God through our spirits and to develop a committed relationship with Him by spend-ing quiet time alone in prayer and worship. As we grow we will become just as confident in God's word as we are that the seasons will change, and as certain as we are that Sunday is before Monday. I have to remind myself often of who I am, not that I'm unsure, but the world will have us to believe that we are all nobody's, from no place, and going no where. When we truly look at the awesomeness of who we are, and how God values our existence we can better understand our true identity. Let's examine what the word says,

"So God created man in His own image; in the image of God He created him; male and female He created them," (Genesis 1:27). Yes, He created us to be reflections of Himself, the very essence of God. "God is Love," (1 John 4:8). He says "You shall be holy; for I am holy," (Leviticus 11:44b). "Therefore you shall be perfect, just as your Father in heaven is perfect," (Matthew 5:48.) Perfect in this sense doesn't mean that you have no sin, but rather being spiritually mature, Christ like, and holy.

"And the Lord God formed man of the dust of the ground, and breathed into his nostrils the breath of life; and man became a living being," (Genesis 2:7). God didn't breathe His breath into animals, insects, birds or any other creatures. We can be assured that we are the elite of all He had created. His own image and His breath inside of us is the seal that He would use to set us apart. When I begin to comprehend that my Creator formed me from the inside out, and that He protected me in my mother's womb; when I gave thought to the fact that I am fearfully and wonderfully made and skillfully wrought; when I comprehended, that God filled me with His substance, even before I was formed, that He actually made the days for me, and not me for the days; when I learned that His thoughts of me were precious and so often, that if I could count them they would be more in number than the grains of sand, (Psalm 139:13–18). This knowledge caused me to value myself, and to value others as God does. When we consider again all that God has done in His creation; and when we think of the magnitude of His all knowing, all powerful magnificence—who are we, that God would keep His mind on us? Who are we that He would make us only a little lower than angels, and have crowned us with glory and honor. He has placed us above the work He had created with His hands. Yes, He has placed us in charge of it all, (Psalm 8). If this isn't enough love for you, He continues to bestow us with honor. "For God so loved the world that He gave His only begotten Son, that whoever believes in Him should not perish but have everlasting life," (John 3:16). Our intended purpose from the beginning was to fellowship with God for eternity. God sent His Son, Jesus, into the world to sacrifice His own life so that our relationship with Him would be restored. Sin separated us from God and before Jesus our only means of communicating with Him was through priests, (Leviticus 16).

Jesus died in the place of each and every one of us, and although He never sinned He became sin for you and me. "For He made Him who knew no sin to be sin for us, that we might become the righteousness of God in Him,"(2 Corinthians 5:21). Jesus was God both in essence and in nature though in human form. He was an extension of God much like our children are extensions of us. God could not have come as Himself, we would not have been able to withstand His glorious presence. Jesus Himself proclaimed. "I and My Father are one," (John 10:30). Yes, because Jesus died we have the wonderful opportunity of approaching God for ourselves, through Him. When we have accepted Christ into our lives, the

Holy Spirit will help us to become Christ like. "But you are a chosen generation, a royal priesthood, a holy nation, His own special people, that you may proclaim the praises of Him who called you out of darkness into His marvelous light," (1 Peter 2:9).

Jesus asks us, "Let not your heart be troubled; you believe in God, believe also in Me. In My Father's house are many mansions; if it were not so, I would have told you. I go to prepare a place for you. And if I go and prepare a place for you, I will come again, and receive you to Myself; that where I am, there you may be also," (John 14:1–3). Jesus said He will come to get us; "Thomas said to Him, 'Lord, we do not know where You are going, and how can we know the way?' Jesus answered, 'I am the way, the truth, and the life. No one comes to the Father except through Me.'" (John 14:5–6). Faith in Jesus is the only way.

If we have faith in the word of the Lord then our faith should proclaim our future and we should be clothed with the garments of salvation and be covered in the robe of righteousness in preparation for our bridegroom (Jesus) to return, (Isaiah 61:10).

Jesus used this story about the ten virgins to illustrate the state of His people upon His return; Jesus explained that ten virgins came to meet their bridegroom all ten had lanterns. Five of them brought extra oil along with their lanterns, and five did not. The bridegroom was delayed and the ten virgins fell asleep. When they awoke, it was at night and their lamps were running out of oil so those who did not bring extra oil asked the other virgins to share their oil with them, and were refused. When the bridegroom finally came in the midnight hour the five virgins had gone to buy oil, and the bridegroom took the five who were prepared with Him to the wedding. When the others returned and saw that the bridegroom had come and taken the virgins they knocked on the door and the bridegroom did not open the door, but answered saying, "I do not know you,"(Matthew 25:1–12). We do not know the day nor the hour that our Lord will come. We must each take responsibility to develop and maintain a personal relationship with God through Christ. We should not depend on anyone else to maintain our personal relationship because it is personal.

Jesus has already paid the price for our sin with His shed blood.

Now He can offer us the gift of eternal life (heaven) to you and to me. Yes heaven is absolutely free; no payments need to be made. There is no amount of work you can do for Him to earn this gift. The Bible says, "For by grace you have been saved through faith, and that not of yourselves; it is the gift of God, not of works, lest anyone should boast," (Ephesians 2:8–9). I've heard many people ask, "If eternal life (heaven) is a free gift, then there is no reason to be good if we can receive it without being good?" The reason why we're good is to show our appreciation and gratitude for what Jesus has already done for us. The entire Bible was written because God wants us to know: "These things have been written to you who believe in the name of the Son of God, that you may know that you have eternal life, and that you may continue to believe in the name of the Son of God." (1 John 5:13). Believing is to trust, we're not talking about knowing of Jesus or even just believing because we read in the Bible that the demons believe and even tremble. (James 2:19). Believing means to trust, "Most assuredly, I say to you, he who believes in Me has everlasting life," (John 6:47). The Bible didn't say that you might have or think you have eternal life, it says "has everlasting life, heaven, eternal life" and this restores us to our intended purpose before sin, we will live with our Creator and with Jesus for eternity. We must connect with "the image of God that lives within us,"(Genesis 1:27). "Behold, I stand at the door and knock. If anyone hears My voice and opens the door. I will come in to him and dine with him, and he with Me," (Revelation 3:20). This news surpasses any news you have ever heard or ever will hear.

Let me tell you how you can receive this gift of Eternal life. I'll make it clear. If you have believed that doing work for the Lord will get you to heaven, it can not. If you have ever depended on the good you do, or the kind words that you have for others; if you believe that going to church every Sunday for service, or shouting in the aisle will get you to heaven, you are mistaken. For all the things that you have trusted in, you must now transfer that trust from what you are doing to get there, and put all of your trust in Christ and Christ alone. "For by grace you have been saved through faith, and that not of yourselves; it is the gift of God, not of works, lest anyone should boast," (Ephesians 2:8–9). You must be ready to receive the living Christ as your personal Savior, and Lord? You must be ready to repent of your sins, to turn all of them to Jesus. If all of the above is true then this is my prayer for you.

> Dear Lord, I ask that you bless all who have wholeheartedly repented of their sins. I ask you Lord to give them saving faith. In the name of Jesus, Amen

This prayer is for you to pray for yourself:

> Father God, I know that I'm a sinner, please forgive me for my sins. I know that Jesus died on the cross and paid the penalty for my sin that I may have eternal life. Live Your life inside of me, and be my personal Savior. I thank You, Father, in the name of Jesus, Amen.

This is my prayer for all who have just accepted Christ as their personal Savior, or have made a new commitment to Him.

> Father, May the Holy Spirit grant assurance to all who have prayed this prayer, give them assurance that they have eternal life. Raise others who will pray for them and with them in the name of Jesus, Amen.

"Most assuredly, I say to you, he who believes in Me has everlasting life," (John 6:47).

Congratulations and welcome to the family of God! Call someone and share the good news that you have accepted Jesus as your personal Savior. The next step in your personal relationship with Jesus is to find a Bible based church that teaches that Jesus is the Son of God. Begin to pray and ask Jesus to guide you, and ask other believers to keep you in prayer too. Stay in fellowship with other believers.

Participate in your new church home Bible study and read the Bible, start with the book of John and read a little at a time. If you don't understand something ask questions until you do. Make your personal relationship with Jesus a priority in your life, and experience the life you were created for in fellowship with God.

My testimony is complete with many storms, but it is a testimony of an awesome God who provided a Son to stand between our sinfulness and Him so that He may see us as He originally created us to be. We are His most precious and elite creation. My faith in Christ has been the supernatural stronghold of my life. I learned to use my trials and tribulations as a means to grow closer to Him, and my prayer is that we do not lose sight of what we've been ordained to do, which is to grow in faith and spiritual maturity. We must prepare the bride which is (the church), to be ready when the bridegroom (Jesus) comes to receive her. "That He might present her to Himself a glorious church, not having spot or wrinkle or any such thing, but that she should be holy and without blemish, (Ephesians 5:27). I am a warrior and I have many battle scars, some are physical, some mental, and there are some emotional ones as well. These scars represent God's victory over the gaping wounds that were once there and are now healed by the blood, love and strength of our Savior Christ Jesus. Faith is the key that will open the gates of heaven.

> "That the genuineness of your faith, being much more precious than gold that perishes, though it is tested by fire, may be found to praise, honor, and glory at the revelation of Jesus Christ, whom having not seen you love. Though now you do not see Him, yet believing, you rejoice with joy inexpressible and full of glory, receiving the end of your faith—the salvation of your souls." (1 Peter 1:7–9)

With You

No matter the obstacle in this life,
No matter the turmoil or the strife.
I'll stand firm because You will be there,
You won't give me more than I can bear.
Whatever in life that I may go through,
I won't mind as long as I face it with you.

My Father the Rock

My Father has laid my path beyond what I can see;
He has already determined when or where I should
be. I will follow the road that He has sent,
No matter the paths, straight or bent.
God had promised to take care of me. And at the
end of the road I will be free. I will walk with
God hand in hand, until I reach His holy land.
I will pray that I keep my Father's clock and
I'll lay my soul upon my Father, the Rock.

VICTORIOUS!

Every single minute of our lives is an opportunity to choose to walk with God. He is always waiting with outstretched arms to embrace His children with love, protection and instruction. We must constantly remember our true identity in Christ; we are a royal priesthood, a holy nation. We are heirs to the throne and we are the reason the world was created. God breathed life into us and His breath caused us to become living beings, (Genesis 2:7); how do we expect to live if we omit Him from our lives? "For we are His workmanship, created in Christ Jesus for good works, which God prepared before hand," (Ephesians 2:10).

There was a time when I believed that dancing, riding a bicycle and walking were gifts from God. Now I understand that they are very human things that we get accustomed to, they're what I call physical luxuries. So often we take for these luxuries for granted. Although they're wonderful blessings they were all to please my own self. What pleases me now is to bring honor to God, to grow in Christ, and to please others. I learned to comfort others while lying flat on my back in excruciating pain and suffering. The more I focused on others, the stronger I became because my focus wasn't on myself but on them. I realize now that this helped me to get through some really tough times. Today I concern myself with what concerns God, which is the salvation of His people. I make sure that as I represent Him that the glory and honor belong to Him.

I've learned that the true evidence of God's logic can only be found through faith, which is the supernatural order of God, along with obedience to His word. There we will find wisdom, under-standing and knowledge.

- "For wisdom is better than rubies, and all things one may desire cannot be compared with her," (Proverbs 8:11).

- "Counsel is mine, and sound wisdom; I am understanding, I have strength..."(Proverbs 8:14).

- "Receive my instruction, and not silver, and knowledge rather than choice gold," (Proverbs 8:10).

- "As long as I have Christ living within me and I have what He has given me, wisdom, understanding and knowledge. If my Spirit is revealing its fruit: love joy, peace, longsuffering, kindness, goodness, faithfulness, gentleness, and self control. (Galatians 5:22–23).

I'd rather be filled with these substances of God than be able to walk physically the whole world over remaining empty. Because of these attributes we can live holy lives in the righteousness of God, and this is all before we enter Eternal Life. From the first book of the Bible to the last, God demonstrates how He will reward us for obedience, faithfulness and for changing our lives by choosing not to live in our sinfulness.

When we allow the Holy Spirit to guide and to lead us, "Now, therefore, you are no longer strangers and foreigners, but fellow citizens with the saints and members of the household of God," (Ephesians 2:19). There's comfort in knowing that we belong to the household of God, and that we are co-heirs to His throne, (Romans 8:17), coming to the realization that we are somebody and that no matter what we may go through in this life we belong to the Most High God, the Creator of heaven and earth. "For this I consider that the sufferings of this present time are not worthy to be compared with the glory which shall be revealed to us," (Romans 8:18).

If my experience in the Comfort Zone was any hint or glimpse of what is awaiting me, these are things confirmed in His word. "The city had no need of the sun or of the moon to shine in it, for the glory of God illuminated it. The Lamb is its light,"(Rev. 21:23). "There shall be no night there; they need no lamp nor light of the sun, for the Lord God gives them light. And they shall reign forever and ever," (Rev. 22:5). The soft but brilliant glow that illuminated me and the overwhelming love that filled me with the Holy Spirit times one billion; voices so indescribably beautiful, which seemed to come from everything, and everywhere praising God to the Highest. "And he showed me a pure river of life clear as crystal…" (Revelation 22:1). If these are any indication of what eternal life holds for me then I will live for God without doubt so that my destiny is sealed. Here we are in this life with an opportunity to experience an eternity with God, remembering all that we've learned about God and considering His love for us, that His thoughts of us would be more than the number of grains of the sand. Who are we indeed? We are His children, His chosen who have endured. We are extensions of our Father, our Creator. Every step we take towards righteousness and holiness is a step towards perfection, a step towards purity and a step towards eternal life.

God used men to bring His word to others through visions, dreams and prophecy. Only the Creator of the world could have such accuracy in predicting in some cases what would come many, many generations ahead. From the promise of the prophet who Moses said would come, (Deuteronomy 18:15); to the covenant God made with Abraham that by his seed all the nations of the earth would be blessed, (Genesis 22:18); from the prophecy which foretold from what country Jesus would come from, (Hosea 11:1). To every prophecy that describes Jesus' life, His death, His resurrection, His ascension and the promise of the Holy Spirit—God is faithful to every promise.

John was one of the Disciples of Christ, the one who Jesus loved. John was prepared to do the work of the Lord because He was a witness to all Jesus taught and ministered. Jesus prophesied to Peter. "Most assuredly, I say to you, when you were younger, you girded yourself and walked where you wished; but when you are old, you will stretch out your hands, and another will gird you and carry you where you do not wish," (John 21:18).

> This He spoke signifying by what death that Peter would glorify God. And when He had spoken this, He said to him, "Follow Me." Then Peter, turning around saw the disciple whom Jesus loved following, who also had leaned on His breast at the supper, and said, "Lord, who is the one who betrays You?" Peter, seeing him, said to Jesus, "But Lord, what about this man?" Jesus said to him, "If I will that he remain till I come, what is that to You? You

follow Me." Then this saying went out among the brethren that this disciple would not die. Yet Jesus did not say to him that he would not die but, "If I will that he remain till I come, what is that to you?" (John 21:19–23)

Jesus' words were misunderstood and the rumors began. God's word is His word! Two things are very important in this scripture. First, the thought of dying on the cross must have frightened Peter, but Jesus told him, "Follow Me." Peter did follow Jesus by feeding His sheep. Peter's ministry involved many healings while building the church of God. Ultimately Peter died on the cross just as Jesus prophesied. Peter was the "rock" on which Jesus began to build the church, (Matthew 16:18). The second thing I noticed is that Peter immediately wanted to know that if he was to die on the cross then, what about John? We have a tendency to concern ourselves with the affairs of others when we should be concentrating on ourselves and what we need to do. Jesus reprimanded Peter, "What is that to you?" This was Jesus' plan for two men devoted to following him. Just because John out lived Peter it didn't mean that Peter's work wasn't as important as John's, but just that John's work was not yet completed. Again both ministries would build and enlarge the church and bring salvation to the people.

God kept John for years as people sought to kill Christians, he was protected for his purpose had not yet been fulfilled. Years passed as John held on to his relationship with his Savior. This is the same John: "When Jesus therefore saw His mother and the disciple whom He loved standing by, He said to His mother, 'Woman, behold your son!' Then He said to the disciple, 'Behold your mother!' And from that hour that disciple took her to his own home," (John 19:26–27).

This John was alive and well in a prison on the island of Patmos. The only living apostle of Jesus, John now an elderly man, is used by Jesus to deliver "The Revelation," which completes the promises of God. The Book of Revelation is a chilling, glorious and victorious message of what awaits us at the end of the age. John is led by visions to the last days of the earth as we have come to know it; there's a fierce battle between good and evil, which ends with God's final victory over the enemy, where we who have overcome the sins of the world are finally changed and perfected. "Behold, I am coming quickly! Hold fast what you have that no one may take your crown," (Revelation 3:11). We must be prepared for His arrival whenever that may be, so that on that glorious day of the Lord. "When Christ who is our life appears, then you will also appear with Him in glory," (Colossians 3:4).

Yes glory, when we will stand before our awesome God to receive the inheritance which was promised to those who loved the Lord with all their hearts, and all their souls and all their minds. Who have believed in the life, death and resurrection of Christ our Savior. "And behold, I am coming quickly and My reward is with Me, to give to every one according to his work," (Revelation 22:12).

"And God will wipe away every tear from their eyes; there shall be no more death, no sorrow, nor crying, there shall be no more pain, for the former things have passed away," (Revelation. 21:4). Jesus promises,

> "He who overcomes I will make him a pillar in the temple of My God, and he shall go out no more. I will write on him the name of My God and the name of the city of My God, the New Jerusalem, which comes down out of heaven from My God. And I will write on him My new name. He who has an ear, let him hear what the Spirit says to the churches." (Revelation 3:12–13)

- "Be faithful until death, and I will give you the crown of life," (Revelation 2:10b).

- "He who overcomes shall be clothed in white garments, and I will not blot out his name from the Book of Life; but I will confess his name before My Father and before His angels," (Revelation 3:5).

- "…To him who overcomes I will give some of the hidden manna to eat. And I will give him a white stone, and on the stone a new name written which no one knows except him who receives it," (Revelation 2:17).

- "And I will give him the morning star," (Revelation 2:28).

- "To him who overcomes I will grant to sit with Me on My throne, as I also overcame and sat down with My Father on His throne. He who has an ear let him hear what the Spirit says to the churches,"(Revelation 3:21–22).

And what was taken away in the beginning,

> "Therefore the Lord God sent him out of the garden of Eden to till the ground from which he was taken. So he drove out the man; and He placed cherubim at the east of the Garden of Eden, and a flaming sword which turned every way, to guard the way to the tree of life." (Genesis 3:23–24)

Yes, the tree that was forbidden in the Garden of Eden because of our sin will again be available to God's children because the New Jerusalem will be sinless.

- "To Him who overcomes I will give to eat from the tree of life, which is in the midst of the Paradise of God," (Revelation 2:7).

- "I am the living bread which came down from heaven. If anyone eats of this bread, he will live forever; and the bread that I shall give is My flesh, which I shall give for the life of the world," (John 6:51).

- "But whoever drinks of the water that I shall give him will never thirst. But the water that I shall give him will become in him a fountain of water springing up into everlasting life," (John 4:14).

Jesus speaks life into us in all that He has taught through His own testimony and accepting Him as the "Bread of life and the Water of Life," we will be included in the book of life and therefore will enter into eternal life to freely eat from the Tree of life. "Then He who sat on the throne said, Behold, I make all things new." And He said to me, "Write, for these words are true and faithful," (Revelation 21:5).

John completed his work for the Lord by recording The Revelation,
Let us also be prepared!

We Thank You

We honor and praise Your holy name,
For this gift of life a home to claim.
A promised future for all to endure,
We're humbled because Your love is pure.
Out of Your splendor and merciful heart,
You have made us worthy of a new start.
When the Struggle's Over
When the struggle's over there will be
glory for us all, who have followed
Jesus as we heard His call. The
gates of heaven will open; He'll
let His children in, No more
pain or suffering and certainly no
sin. Jesus, thank You for Your
blessings and thank You for Your
love, and when the struggle's over
we'll meet You up above.

"My Sheep Hear My Voice…

and I know them and they follow Me. And I give them
eternal life, and they shall never perish; neither shall
anyone snatch them out of My hand. My Father, who
has given them to Me, is greater than all; and no one
is able to snatch them out of My Father's hand."
(John 10:27–29)

LEARNING TO HEAR GOD

AFTER ACCEPTING CHRIST AS YOUR PERSONAL SAVIOR, learning to hear God's voice requires you to have a personal relationship with Jesus. It's the only way to communicate with God. A relationship involves participation from two or more parties.

Jesus said to him, "I am the way, the truth, and the life. No one comes to the Father except through Me."

John 14:6

When you accept Jesus as your personal Savior you will also receive the Holy Spirit.

"But the Helper, the Holy Spirit, whom the Father will send in My name, He will teach you all things, and bring to your remembrance all things that I said to you."

John 14:26

Now He who has prepared us for this very thing is God, who also has given us the Spirit as a guarantee.

2 Corinthians 5: 18–20

It's guaranteed!

Make a commitment to read, and to study Jesus' life from the book of John in your Bible. Read a little at a time.

I beseech you therefore, of God, that you present your bodies a living sacrifice, holy acceptable to God, which is your reasonable service.

Romans 12:1

Not just in word, but in deed. Prayer is the main line to talk to God, in Jesus' name:

> Lord God,
> I ask You to guide me in my relationship with You. Lead me as I turn my life over to You now. Please help me to

become who You have created me to be. Make Your word clear to me, and help me to live Your word.

In the name of Jesus, Amen.

After prayer, spend quiet time with Jesus alone, no radio, no television, no telephone, no computer and no other distractions, just you and Him. Close your eyes and meditate on His name, His love and the many blessings He has given you. Thank Him for dying in your place on the cross. The more time you spend with Him, the more opportunities you give yourself to hear His voice.

In diligent prayer, study, obedience, worship and meditation you will be allowed to enter the holiest of holies. This is a supernatural place of peace, rest, and communion with the Lord. Spiritually you will glow in His presence. In this supernatural relationship His voice will become clear, precise, and unmistakable.

EPILOGUE

Sharing bits of my testimony was usually one on one with the new members of my church. The fragment I shared most often was coming from paralysis after twenty-seven years. I understand now that healing began on the inside immediately. I also realize that I needed every single moment of those years to gain the character, the patience and experience to serve Him unconditionally.

In my relationship with Christ I can look back through my life recognizing God's power, how it was a carefully orchestrated symphony that when all played together is another beautiful, loving and tremendous testimony of His faithfulness. The reason He sent Christ to die for us, is so that no matter what we may endure, it will be all to His glory. I stand in awe of His meticulous and wonderful movement in my life, which allows me to clearly see this movement in all of His creation. I pray to be a faithful student so that I may be the kind of witness that Paul and Moses, David and Daniel have been. Because I work hard to reflect God's image I find myself without effort concerning myself with what concerns God. My mind reflects the thoughts of Christ through the Holy Spirit. God's concern for His people is most important to Him. It grieves God that even one of us shall be lost. He created us to live with Him eternally. It grieves my own spirit as I watch the news. We are constantly barraged with total rebellion against God. The enemy uses media to numb us so that rebellion against God is acceptable. He wants our children to be numb towards murder and violence; great care is placed in convincing them that it's alright and he uses the very things that will attract them to his deception, video games, movies, TV shows, and music.

We choose to remain sinful in the sight of God because we're not taught to fear Him, and because of the lack of a personal relationship with Jesus. It takes effort and will power to overcome sin. Many of us are not willing to do the work it takes to live the life we were created to live, but once you have mastered it you will be resting on God's power, and not your own power. I wanted to shout all that I have heard and learned and overcome from the rooftops. That's how I wanted to do it, but God decided that it would be in this form. This began as an autobiography, today it is a testimony of an awesome God. I've kept diaries and have collected hospital records. Poems, some of which were written thirty years ago, have a place in this memoir. Only God could have orchestrated these things so perfectly.

God has given me such a wonderful and fulfilling life, that if I ceased to walk right this minute I would still have awesome faith in the Lord. The miracles in my life have been overwhelming and they have already been performed and nothing can take that away. I stay grounded by knowing who I am and to whom I belong. During my first open heart surgery I came home with a scar in the shape of the letter "T," and after the last opened heart surgery the "T" became a cross with an extra line above the "T." I use this as a reminder of what Jesus has done for me. Both dying in my place and giving me a new life.

Let us commit to a personal relationship with Christ Jesus so that we may do what we have been created to do—live eternally with Christ. We should be clothed in righteousness and be prepared and waiting when the bridegroom (Christ) comes to receive His bride (the church).

> Dear Lord,
> We ask for Your guidance and power in changing our lives. We ask You to strip us of anything that is not of You. We thank You that You have delivered us. Protect us and keep us until You come to receive us.
> In the mighty name of Jesus. Amen.

Let us worship Him in spirit and in truth.

Ventricle Septal Defect or VSD–a hole in the heart, which is caused by the failure of complete twisting and joining of the heart at the time of it's becoming a functioning organ.

Heart Murmur–a heart murmur is a distinctive sound that may sometimes indicate a more serious problem with the heart or its valves. These problems can cause blood to flow abnormally through the valves. Some people have murmurs that are usually not a problem.

Kyphosis–a curvature of the spine which is outward causing a hump.

Scoliosis–a curvature in the spine that is to one side or the other.

Spinal Fusion–a surgical procedure that joins or fuses two or more vertebrae. Bone is taken from pelvic bone and used to make a bridge between adjacent vertebrae.

Bacterial Endocarditis–an infection on one or more valves of the heart.

Tricuspid Valve–a heart valve that help prevents blood from flowing back into the right atrium when the right ventricle contracts.

Scar Tissue–when skin and organs are damaged, the body naturally wants to heal itself. Since the body can not re-create healthy skin or tissue it puts together new fibers that are not as functional as the original tissue, but that serve as a protective and useful barrier. When this barrier is completely healed it is known as scar tissue. It can be found on any tissue, including skin, or internal organs where an injury, cut, surgery or disease has taken place.

Pleura–a thin tissue covering the lung and lining the interior wall of the chest cavity

Bradycardia–slow heart rhythm

Pacemaker–a battery operated electrical device insert into the body to deliver small regular shocks that stimulate the heart to beat in a normal rhythm.

Congestive Heart Failure–a weakened heart muscle that has a hard time keeping up with the demands to pump enough oxygen to supply the body.

Rheumatoid Arthritis–a common disease of the joints, membranes or tissue of the joints the lining of the joints become inflamed over time, the inflammation may destroy joint tissue.

Osteoponea–the loss of bone density that is lower then normal peak, but not low enough to be called osteoporsis.

Osteoporosis–is a progressive disease that causes bone to become thin and brittle, making them more likely to break. It could lead to permanent disability.

Osteoarthritis–a condition in which the cartilage that protects and cushions joints breaks down causing bones to rub together. Most common in the hands, feet, spine and large weight bearing joints such as the hips and knees.

Degenerative Disc Disease–a name to describe the normal wear to your spinal column.

Esophagus–a muscular tube that connects the throat to the stomach.

Transesephageal echocardiogram–a probe is passed down the esophagus instead of being moved over the outside of the chest wall. It shows clearer pictures. The probe is located closer to the heart.

Cardiac Arrest–sudden and abrupt loss of heart function.

Respiratory Arrest–sudden and abrupt loss of lung function.

Resuscitation–a procedure to bring stimulation the heart to cause it to beat.

Nasotracheally Intubated–a tube inserted in the nasal passage and placed in the throat to open the airway.

Adult Respiratory Distress Syndrome (ARDS)–a type of severe acute lung dysfunction affecting all or most of both lungs that occurs as a result of illness or injury. ARDS may develop in conjunction with widespread infection in the body. ARDS is the most severe from of lung injury.

Sepsis–is the body's response to infection. Patients who have sepsis can progress from being ill to seriously ill, to organ dysfunction and failure and then to septic shock to death. People with heart disease have an increased risk of sepsis.

Tracheotomy–cutting into the windpipe to relieve obstruction.

Decubitus–bedsore

Chest tubes–tubes that are inserted into the chest between ribs and into the space between inner lining and the outer lining of the lungs to drain fluid of any kind from the patient to allow full expansion of the lungs.

Post Traumatic Stress Disorder (PSTD)–symptoms which are a result of a traumatic experience that involve the threat of death or serious injury and evoke fear, helplessness or horror. Symptoms include: nightmares, intrusive memories, flashbacks, and physical reactions to anything that serves as a reminder of the experience. What all of these symptoms have in common is an inability to shake off the ruling influence of the traumatic experience.

Chronic Obstructive Pulmonary Disease (COPD)–is a group of long term (chronic) lung diseases that makes it hard to breathe. In COPD, airflow through the airways leading to and within the lungs is partially blocked, resulting difficulty breathing. As the disease gets worse, breathing becomes more difficult. Although COPD can be managed, it can not be cured at this time.

Pulmonary Vein–a large vein that carries blood away from the heart to the body

Diuretic–medication given to eliminate fluid from the body

Nebulizer Treatments–a treatment that delivers liquid medication in the form of the midst to the lungs to help open airways.

Heart Catheterization–a test used to discover abnormalities of the heart.